SOCIETY
and the ASSASSIN

*A Background Book
on Political Murder*

SOCIETY
and the ASSASSIN

A BACKGROUND BOOK
ON POLITICAL MURDER

By Bernhardt J. Hurwood

Parents' Magazine Press • New York

Each Background Book is concerned with the broad spectrum of people, places and events affecting the national and international scene. Written simply and clearly, the books in this series will engage the minds and interests of people living in a world of great change.

To my wife, Laura, whose patience, understanding, and valued assistance during the birth pangs, childhood, and maturation of this book made the difficult times endurable, and the exciting ones an adventure worth sharing.

CONTENTS

LIST OF ILLUSTRATIONS

Illustrations follow page 124

AUTHOR'S PREFACE

Although no book has ever written itself, some of them have a strange way of taking their authors by the hand, as it were, and steering them into totally unexpected areas. This is exactly what happened here. Originally I had intended to write a book about a single political murder. It was to be an in-depth study of Daniel Mc-Naughton, the psychotic Scot who attempted to assassinate British Prime Minister Sir Robert Peel in 1843. But the McNaughton case led elsewhere, and after being hopelessly diverted from my original course, McNaughton was relegated to a single chapter.

What now began taking shape was a long-range historical examination of the relationship between society and the assassin. This provided a perfect title, but threatened to reach encyclopedic proportions. There was only one way to avoid this. That was to approach the subject in such a way as to offer a solid foundation for anyone wishing to pursue it at greater length. Consequently there are many well-known assassination events that are mentioned here superficially or not at all. It seemed more important to remain within the framework of that all-important relationship between the assassins and the societies that spawned them.

I have touched on such diverse but related matters as political terrorism, extremism, philosophical attitudes toward assassination, organized crime, the mass media, and the rhetoric of violence. Happily I was able to draw profitably upon the diligent scholarship, journalism, and expert opinion of others past and present. Hopefully I will have succeeded in shedding some much-needed light on the curious paradox that exists in man; that the most intelligent of all creatures on earth, the one who most loves life because he is sentient, is the most destructive of life.

1

THE
RIGHTEOUS ASSASSINS

At one time the term "assassin" was applied rather loosely to anyone who committed an act of premeditated murder. What generally distinguished assassination from ordinary homicide, however, was an assumption that the assassin acted on behalf of others, or out of fanatical devotion to some cause or faith. Consequently, despite religious and cultural injunctions against killing, there have always been circumstances in which society (or certain segments of it) has condoned homicide, which has frequently been followed by loud cheers of public approval. Aside from judicial killing, however, there has rarely been much agreement as to what, if anything, constitutes justifiable homicide.

Among civilized peoples it is held that lawfully constituted governmental agencies are the only ones possessing the right to impose judicial homicide or capital punishment. Enlightened societies are gradually abandoning capital punishment, but there is no guarantee that with its abolition potential assassins will suddenly vanish into thin air. Everywhere in the world there are individuals

and groups who, from time to time, take it upon themselves to assume the duties of judge, jury, and executioner
by slaying people—usually public figures—for reasons they
consider legitimate. Throughout history murder has been a
decisive political tool—a drastic one, to be sure, but none
the less significant for all its ill repute. This leads directly to the definition of assassination as it will be used
here: willful murder for political, religious, or similar
reasons.

For the purpose of providing a clearer understanding
and broader background to the subject, then, during the
course of the book we shall touch briefly on several related
subjects including human sacrifice, Thuggee (practiced by
an underground confederation of India), vendettas (or blood
feuds), and duelling. Whether we care to admit it or
not, all these violent, bygone institutions cast dim shadows
which still lie dormant within us, and with which we
must cope when they unexpectedly awaken and take us by
surprise. Besides, each clearly illustrates conditions under
which past societies have permitted or insisted upon the
deliberate termination of human life for reasons considered
sound at the time.

Although considerably removed from assassination as
we understand it, human sacrifice was once regarded by
its practitioners as an essential means to a variety of
ends. Angry deities with a penchant for inflicting calamity
appear in retrospect to have been the most insatiable
gluttons for human victims. In societies where the practice was rife, ordinary people believed firmly that human
sacrifice would ensure against such elemental catastrophes
as flood, earthquake, famine, and fire. On the other hand,
they were led to believe that it could be equally effective
in producing military victories and other desired ends.

Victims rarely had anything to say in the matter, although we find occasional accounts of individuals voluntarily offering themselves. Usually they were chosen arbitrarily, and as often as not dragged off kicking and screaming in bitter protest. In certain cultures these sacrificial victims were permitted to live out the short time that remained to them in consummate luxury. But this must have been a minor compensation on the day they were ordained to die.

We can only wonder about the high priests and other officials responsible for the selection process. Did they function as omnipotent draft boards, whose decisions were irrevocable and beyond all appeal? Did they use their power to eliminate real and potential enemies, or did they simply make arbitrary choices? The questions that arise are many and impossible to answer. The study of such historical sidelights as these tends to make cynics out of serious students, especially when they speculate on the inner motives of those who wielded absolute power in matters of life and death. When Mao Tse-tung wrote that all power comes from the barrel of a gun, he was merely reiterating an ancient principle that has been abused more often than not.

The logical starting point for an examination of the often complex interrelationship between society and the assassin is with the origin of the term itself. There are several theories, none of which can be proven conclusively. One holds that the word "assassin" is derived from the Arabic root *Hassa,* meaning, among other things, to kill or to exterminate. Another offers quite a different explanation, suggesting another Arabic word, *Asas,* meaning an *Imam,* or holy man associated with a prophet. Still another speculates that it is derived from a word meaning "Followers of Hassan" (specifically Hassan ibn-al-Sabbah, whose story follows). The most common belief is an oversimplification, namely that "assassin" derives from the Arabic *Hashishin,* meaning "users of hashish." In all probability, crusaders brought back the corrupted Latinization of the word *assassinus,* from which it eventually took its various European forms. They used hashish in a very special way (as we shall see presently), but so did non-Assassins. Therefore, any assumption that the original Assassins were nothing more than an undisciplined gang of drug-maddened murderers, running amok and killing everyone in sight, is sheer nonsense. As is generally known, the Koran specifically prohibits the use of wine. Early Moslems, like other human beings, enjoyed the escape or the exhilaration provided by intoxicants, but in order to obey their holy writ, substitutes had to be found for the juice of the fermented grape. Who first discovered hashish is unimportant, but it is known that it came into use at a very early stage of history.

To present the story of the original Assassins with any degree of validity, it is first necessary to wipe away the prejudiced coloring smeared on the pages of history by so many early writers. Above all they were a politico-religious sect spawned by the bitter factional strife that fragmented Islam after the death of the Prophet Mohammed. Writing of this in terms of Mohammed's farsighted perception of the future, nineteenth-century historian von Hammer-Purgstall wrote:

> . . . it had not escaped him, that in the constant progress of history there is nothing immutable; that no human institution can be endowed with perpetual duration, and that the spirit of one gen-

eration seldom survives that which succeeds it. It was in this sense
that he said, prophetically, "The caliphate will last only thirty
years after my death."[1]

Although the caliphate, or true line of succession, was
the root of all controversy, Islam as a religious faith was
no more weakened by factional strife than was Christianity,
centuries later, by the Protestant Reformation. The outcome, however, was obvious. Since the position of the
caliph embodied what in Europe would have combined
the offices of pope, emperor, and divine prophet, it offered
unlimited wealth and power to its possessor—especially
power. What this fragmentation of Islam resulted in was
the mushrooming of different sects. Each recognized
Mohammed as the true Prophet of Allah, the Koran as
the true scripture. Although approximately seventy-two
different sects sprang up, they fit into one or the other
of two major subdivisions: the Sunnites, who believed in
orthodoxy, and recognized one line of succession, and the
Shiites, who recognized another. In time the Shiites adopted
many pre-Islamic concepts and became more identified
with non-Arab Moslems, and it was from the bosom of
Shiism that the Order of the Assassins was eventually to
spring.

The sect that would one day be known as the Assassins
broke away from Shiism, around the year 760 A.D., over
another dispute involving rightful succession. They called
themselves Ismailis, after Ismail, son of Jafar al-Sadiq,
great-grandson of Ali and Fatima, through whom they
traced the Prophet's legitimate descendants.

The Ismailis' beliefs differed so radically from those of
conventional Shiism that in time they were forced to go
underground. Being far from passive, however, they spread
their doctrine with fiery zeal over the length and breadth

of Islam. The more they proselytized, the more converts
they gained. Thus, in the year 969, with a triumphal
sweep they seized Egypt and founded an Ismaili dynasty
which came to be known as the Fatimid Caliphate, after
Fatima, daughter of Mohammed.

They selected for their capital an old garrison town on
the Nile, and named it El-Kahira, meaning "The Vic-
torious." By the eleventh century it had become not only
the center of Islamic culture, but one of the most magnificent cities of the medieval world—Cairo. Like a magnet
it attracted merchants, adventurers, princes, and thieves.
Like a fascinating woman, it held them all in its spell,
infidels and believers alike. Its gleaming palaces and
mosques stood as towering monuments to Islamic crafts-
men and their art. Its teeming bazaars displayed the world's
most fabulous riches—silks from China, spices and jewels
from India, fine steel from Damascus, and slaves of all
colors from Africa, Asia, and Europe.

In the year 1002, the celebrated House of Wisdom was
founded. Combination university, library, and center of
Ismaili missionary activity, it was to attract students from
all of Islam. Hammer-Purgstall tells us that it was

> . . . richly furnished with books, mathematical instruments, pro-
> fessors, and attendants. Access, and the use of these literary treas-
> ures [including nearly 250,000 books] was free to all, and writing
> materials were afforded gratis. The Caliphs frequently held learned
> disputations, at which the professors of the academy appeared,
> divided according to their different faculties—logicians, mathe-
> maticians, jurists, and physicians were dressed in their gala costume,
> *khalaa,* or their doctoral mantles.[2]

It was to the House of Wisdom that a Persian convert
to Ismailiism came in 1078. His name was Hassan ibn-
al-Sabbah. He burned with ambition, and his timing could

not have been more perfect. By now the world of Islam was torn with even greater conflict than before. There were three caliphates, each claiming legitimacy: the Fatimid, whose domain encompassed Egypt, Syria, Algeria, and most of Arabia; the Abbasid (claiming descent from Abbas, an uncle of Mohammed and Ali), which ruled Baghdad and its environs; and the Ommiad, which, after being defeated by the Abbasids in 750 A.D., had licked its wounds, regrouped, and established itself again in Spain and Morocco. Arabs, Berbers, Persians, and Turks engaged in continuous struggles, while on the sectarian level, Ismailis, Shiites, and Sunnites (the strict orthodox sect) bitterly opposed one another in never-ending disputes over the fine points of religious observance.

Hassan ibn-al-Sabbah, whose exact birthdate is unknown, came into the world some time after Macbeth murdered Duncan in Scotland, halfway around the world. He was born in Rey, a flourishing city at the time, which today is nothing more than a suburb of Tehran. It is known that Hassan was the son of a Shiite merchant who was forced to observe his faith clandestinely because of Sunnite persecution, that he was a brilliant youth, and that he was eventually converted to Ismailiism after an initial opposition to its doctrines. That he possessed an insatiable thirst for knowledge is definitely known, and when we consider that the Ismaili concept of Heaven was perfect wisdom, and Hell, total ignorance, we get an inkling as to why the man was attracted to the sect.

There is a legend about him which tells that he studied in the Persian city of Nishapur under a celebrated imam named Mowaffek, along with Omar Khayyam and Nizam-al-Mulk (later grand vizier of the Turkoman empire). According to the story, the three youths became fast friends and swore an oath that the first one to achieve success would assist the other two. This was in keeping with the belief that all pupils of the great imam were destined to achieve greatness. Whether the three were actually friends, or even students of Mowaffek, hardly matters, for each eventually attained the pinnacle of success.

Hassan rose rapidly in the hierarchy of the Ismailis. In 1078, when he went to Cairo, turmoil in Islam was approaching the boiling point. The Persian Ismailis began to doubt the strength of the Fatimid Caliphate. The Turks and the Abbasids were struggling for supremacy, and against this background Hassan began developing ideas of his own. He cultivated a deep distrust of those who did not share his beliefs. He plunged into political intrigues, irrevocably mixed with religious proselytizing, developing along the way a precise policy of his own.

His followers were imbued with a degree of loyalty seldom seen before or since. Absolute, blind faith coupled with equally absolute obedience was required. He did not set himself up as a caliph or imam, but he did make it clear that he was the direct link to the rightful descendant of the True Prophet. So charismatic, so convincing was he, that by the year 1090 he had gathered a formidable band of followers, and was able to seize the fortress of Alamut in a bloodless takeover. There is no better description of it than that of Enno Franzius, who wrote:

> In the bleak, melancholy, almost lunar Elburz mountains there is a remote valley enclosed by steep slopes. Through it flows the Alamut River. A stream, the Kasir, issues into it from the north. At the head of this tributary's vale about two hours' walk from the Alamut, rises a rocky gray eminence with sheer sides. It is 600 feet high, 450 feet long, and 30 to 125 feet wide, and is partly encompassed by the towering Elburz range. Other than a narrow neck to a lava monticle between it and the Elburz, it has no junction with the circumjacent landscape. On this unassailable site,

often circled by eagles and reached by almost perpendicular steps crudely hacked out of the rock, stood an impregnable castle, to which centuries before an eagle was believed to have guided its builder—Alamut (Eagle's Guidance).[3]

Once he had the fortress, Hassan made Alamut the headquarters of his own version of Ismailiism, which went off in its unique way to become a sub-sect of the original. It is said that never again did he set foot outside, except upon two occasions when he ventured out to the parapets. Ruling his followers with an iron hand, he instituted some of the most bizarre but effective indoctrination methods ever conceived by anyone.

It should be noted here that the reason for Hassan's diversion from the main branch of Ismailiism was no different from that offered by others before him—line of succession. He held to the opinion that Prince Nizar of the Fatimid Caliphate was the rightful successor. But the ill-fated Nizar was the victim of a political intrigue and was imprisoned and murdered in 1095. For this reason— Hassan's recognition of Nizar—his followers are called Nizaris by some writers.

Hassan ibn-al-Sabbah, recognizing that power was most speedily attained by murdering those who stood in his way, firmly believed that such murders were justified. Furthermore, as one who believed in absolute autocracy, he had no faith in or respect for the common man. He believed that the masses were best led by a tightly controlled elite who gave allegiance to a divinely appointed leader. This was loosely in keeping with Ismaili doctrine, in which the masses were permitted to practice more or less orthodoxy in their religious observance as long as they followed the leadership of the elite.

Where Hassan differed from traditional Ismailiism was in his *modus operandi*. Intelligent youths, chosen for their

enthusiasm, faith, resourcefulness, and good health were
organized into a novitiate called the *Fida'is,* meaning
"devout ones," "disciples," or "the faithful." They were
taught the principles of the faith (as interpreted by Hassan),
which included the necessity for blind obedience and
unshakable loyalty. Of equal importance was their com-
mando-like training in the art of murder by stealth, utiliz-
ing every means imaginable—poison, the blade, the garrote,
and bare hands.

Most fascinating is the method by which Hassan is supposed to have made himself absolute master of his followers. It was based upon the traditional Moslem concept
of paradise, which differed from the Christian mainly in
that it appealed to the sensual aspirations rather than to the
spiritual, although it by no means excluded the latter.

Using as prime source the account written by Marco
Polo, who referred to Hassan as "The Old Man of the
Mountain" (see Document I), a French authority, Sylvestre
de Sacy, wrote in 1809:

> The whole of their education [the *Fida'is*] went to convince them
> that, by blindly obeying the orders of their chief, they insured to
> themselves, after death, the enjoyment of every pleasure that can
> flatter the senses. For this purpose the prince [Hassan] had de-
> lightful gardens laid out near his palace; there in pavillions,
> decorated with everything rich and brilliant that Asiatic luxury
> can devise, dwelt young beauties, dedicated solely to the pleasure
> of those for whom these enchanting regions were destined. Thither,
> from time to time, the princes of the Ismailites [sic] caused the
> young people, whom they wished to make the blind instruments
> of their will, to be transported. After administering to them a
> beverage which threw them into a deep sleep, and deprived them
> for some time of the use of their faculties, they were carried into
> those pavillions, which were fully worthy of the gardens of Armida*;
> on awakening, everything which met their eyes, or struck their
> ears, threw them into a rapture, which deprived reason of all

control over their minds; and uncertain whether they were still on earth, or whether they had already entered upon the enjoyment of their felicity, the picture of which had so often been presented to their imagination, they yielded in transport to all the kinds of seduction, in which they were surrounded. After they had passed some days in these gardens, the same means which had been adopted to introduce them, without being conscious of it, were made use of to remove them.[4]

The implications of de Sacy's passage are quite clear. Those chosen to serve as *Fida'is* were never intended to rise through the hierarchy, eventually to join the top echelons of leadership. They were shock troops, the expendable pawns, whose ranks could easily be refilled by eager replacements. As for the use of hashish, it was given to them without their knowledge after they had been drugged with something else meant only to make them lose consciousness. Through the continuous use of hashish, most likely administered in liquid form, while they remained in the gardens, they were kept on what would be called in the vernacular today a monumental high, until they were drugged into unconsciousness again and then brought back to the real world where they eventually awakened.

Understandably, when they finally returned to normal, they were convinced beyond a doubt that they had indeed visited paradise, and they *knew* that if they were killed in the course of their activities it would merely hasten their return trip. So carefully was this large-scale deception organized that mothers of young *Fida'is* put on festive attire and celebrated when they received word that their

* A fictional sorceress of great beauty, who lives "in a castle that contains a garden of gorgeous sensual delights, from lush flowers and fruits to alluring nymphs bathing in fountains. It symbolizes the attractions of the senses and their power over human reason." (*Reader's Encyclopedia, pg. 51*)

sons had been killed. But when they learned that their boys had returned alive, they shaved their heads, smeared them with ashes, and donned mourning.

The precision and skill employed by the Assassins as they struck down their assigned targets was too great for them to have been undisciplined fanatics acting under the influence of mind-bending drugs. They were calculating killers carrying out strict orders. Only princes, caliphs, viziers, and other powerful dignitaries had any reason to fear their assaults, since they regarded wanton killing for personal reasons as beneath their dignity.

Hassan ibn-al-Sabbah continued to spread his influence by means of terror, poison, and dagger until he died peacefully of old age in the year 1124. By this time the Assassins had extended their tentacles throughout Islam and enjoyed the peak period of their power, and it was actually during this period that they carried out the most significant assassinations. Eventually their control of Syria became so firm that the need for assassination diminished, and their policies became relatively conventional. But in becoming the established order themselves, they engendered radicalism within their own ranks. The Syrian branch broke away from the main body and many Assassin leaders died at the hands of other Assassins.

In the year 1186 the astrologers of Asia trembled for their lives. The seven known planets were in conjunction in the sign of Libra, convincing them that the end of the world was imminent. But they had miscalculated. Only the end of the Assassins was at hand. The last grand master, Rukn al-Din Khurshah, as a result of poor counsel and his own naiveté, surrendered the fortress of Alamut, the nerve center of Assassin power, to the Mongols, only to be betrayed and to perish at their hands in the midst of a general slaughter in which about 12,000 persons died. The Mongol historian Juvani summed up what happened by writing, "Of him and his stock no trace was left, and he and his kindred became but a tale on men's lips and a tradition in the world." This was not quite accurate, because the Assassins continued to exist. But as a decisive factor in Middle-Eastern politics they were finished, though like a dying dragon, lashing its tail, they engaged in spurts of activity well into the thirteenth century. Thus, though they flourished by the dagger and the poisoned cup, they perished by the sword, after giving a name to the politics of murder forever.

As a footnote to the Assassins, it should be mentioned that the Ismailis still exist, but they are peaceful citizens of many countries throughout the world today, acknowledging as their forty-ninth rightful imam the Aga Khan, Karim, born in 1937, son of Aly Khan and an Englishwoman, Joan Guinness.

Another sect in India conducted a reign of terror which was different from that of the Assassins, but which, like that, contributed a word to the English language. Called Phansigars (literally, "noose operators") by some and Dacoits (from the Hindustani *Dakait,* meaning "members of a gang of robbers") by others, they were best known as Thugs, and were worshippers of the Hindu goddess Kali, goddess of destruction. This last name is derived from Sanskrit and is generally held to mean concealment. There is no more terrible deity in the Hindu Pantheon, and it would be difficult to find a more graphic description of her statue than that which appeared in the *Polytechnic Journal* of London, in September 1840.

> Her attitude is one of fearful threatening, calculated to inspire terror, and this even to the most obsequious of worshippers. The

expression of her countenance is, to the last degree, horrible. Her
eyes are large and projecting; her nose thin, with nostrils greatly
dilated, as if under the immediate influence of intense passion.
The mouth extends nearly the whole width of the face, being
armed with a row of immense teeth, like small hatchets; and from
the upper jaw, at each corner of the extended gums, projects a
short, thick tusk, curling towards the ear on either side, which it
nearly touches. From her mouth, a large, rough tongue protrudes,
and descends to her waist; under it and round her scraggy neck is
entwined a *Cobra di Capello* snake, a deadly reptile, which sup-
ports this monstrous member upon its snaky folds. Beneath each
ear is one of those deadly serpents, hanging from it, as an orna-
mental pendant to this monstrous head. The hood of the snake
is expanded, as if in the act of attack. The ears of the idol are
large, pendulous, and project considerably from the head, greatly
increasing its hideousness of aspect. The body is gaunt and macer-
ated; but the limbs are extremely robust, and all are bent, to
express great energy of action. The hands are gigantic, the fingers
long, and armed with thick, pointed nails, like claws. A serpent
entwines the waist, with the hood extended. No lips cover her
teeth, and the mouth, therefore, grins horribly. Her bloated cheeks
and fierce goggle eyes are fixed, with an appalling stare, upon
the beholder. Her hair is erect, and stiffened out upon her un-
sightly head, forming a frightful glory round it, diverging to meet
a wider glory, which rises from a flower on each side, forming a
support to the figure.

The Thugs existed as an underground confederation all
over India, and came from all walks of life. Their victims
were killed for a twofold reason: religious duty and profit.
Recognizing one another by means of an elaborate system
of secret passwords and signals, they considered themselves exceptionally devout, and practiced their brand of
murder and robbery according to rigidly prescribed ritual.
Generally they would attach themselves to bands of travellers making long journeys across remote sections of
wilderness. They would be charming companions, totally

disarming in their manner, and at night they would enter-
tain the others with songs, stories, and other diversions.
As a rule they would be the first ones to volunteer for
lookout or guard duty at night, which, of course, gave
them a tremendous advantage when the propitious moment came to dispatch their victims.

Travelling in bands of from ten to two hundred, they
operated with military precision. Those who were too old
or infirm to perform strenuous tasks did more prosaic
things like cooking, cleaning, spying, and animal handling.
Like the Assassins, the Thugs were masters of disguise, and
when they embarked on their forays they assumed whatever identities seemed best suited to the occasion. Sometimes they would appear as pilgrims, other times as
merchants, and occasionally even as a prince with a large
entourage. Their main purpose was to give the appearance
of legitimate travellers.

Their rules prohibited indiscriminate killing. Not only
were they forbidden to kill women, but they could not
harm fakirs, bards or musicians, dancers, sweepers, oil
venders, blacksmiths, carpenters (the last two only when
travelling together), lepers, maimed persons, men with
cows, or carriers of water from the River Ganges.

When they did kill, the victims were strangled swiftly
and efficiently with the ritual noose, which was called a
phansi. Then offerings were made to the goddess, including a portion of the goods taken from the murdered
persons, and finally the bodies were disposed of in such
a way as to make certain that they would never be found.
An important reason for the unrivalled success of Thuggee
over so many centuries was the rule which stated that no
victim could be attacked by less than two thugs. This,
coupled with the fact that their techniques were so lethally

efficient, made it impossible for even the strongest individuals to escape.

There is a legend that the very first Thugs never both-
ered to dispose of their victims' bodies because the goddess always came along and attended to the task by
devouring the remains herself. But one day while she was
engaged in her dreadful repast, a follower looked back
and saw her picking the bones. She was so offended that
she vowed never to eat another victim of Thuggee again,
thus forcing the devout to be forever after responsible for
getting rid of the bodies themselves. But in order to
compensate them for the loss of her presence, she gave
them one of her tusks as a pickaxe, one of her ribs as
a knife (the edge of which could never be deflected),
and the hem of her garment as a noose.

One of the best accounts of Thuggee from the inside
and out is in a novel, *The Deceivers,* by John Masters,
which is a fictional, but accurate story of how the British
went about stamping out the sect in the middle 1830's.
Ironically, though they had heard of Thuggee, they
refused to believe, until about 1810, that such a thing
could exist, and even then made no actual moves against
the Thugs until 1830.

To all intents and purposes the Thugs have been gone
completely for over a hundred years. Nevertheless, Kali
is still worshipped in parts of India even today, and there
were reports of Thuggee-type assassinations as late as
the 1940's. But whether the perpetrators were true followers of Kali the Destroyer in the old style, or common
criminals, is a question that for now must remain unanswered.

2

DEATH
to TYRANTS

The original Greek version of the word "tyrant" referred merely to an absolute ruler. Since bitter human experience has taught mankind that absolute rulers of any stripe invariably become harsh and oppressive, the concept of tyranny has taken on the same coloration. So now, when we refer to tyrants, we take it for granted that they are not only powerful rulers, but malignant ones as well.

Throughout history there have been rulers who began their careers in an atmosphere of popular approval which eventually turned to hatred as a direct result of their oppressive rule. Thus in every age a problem has arisen from the simple fact that no tyrant willingly steps down from the seat of power. But when a tyrant goes too far, as they all eventually do, how is he forcibly removed? Since tyrants always make it a point to surround themselves with loyal henchmen, the only way to get rid of them is by assassination (or tyrannicide as it has been called). Remember, we are referring here to the absolute dictator (regardless of what title he bears) who recognizes no authority but his own. When he dies, all authority dies with him, and in the ensuing scramble for power a new tyrant eventually rises, phoenix-like, from the ashes of the last one.

Tyrants have flourished under political systems without built-in guarantees affording the people protection against tyranny by providing for peaceful and orderly succession of power. Consequently, even honest liberators, with lofty ideals and nobility of purpose, have often become tyrants in time. Edmund Burke stated the case succinctly in 1756 when he said, "Power gradually extirpates from the mind every humane and gentle virtue." And less than twenty years later, Abigail Adams wrote to her husband, John, "I am more and more convinced that man is a dangerous creature; and that power, whether vested in many or a few, is ever grasping, and like the grave, cries, 'Give, give!' "

Complex problems have always faced civilized men contemplating tyrannicide in the face of oppression. The basic question is: "Is tyrannicide right?" From this, other questions have sprung up like a harvest of dragons' teeth. Under what conditions is tyrannicide proper? Who has the right to determine these conditions, and, indeed, the justice of the act itself? And though by no means the ultimate question, certainly one of the most important is who decides beyond all doubt that a man is actually a tyrant? When John Wilkes Booth leaped to the stage of Ford's Theater after shooting Abraham Lincoln, he cried out, "Sic semper tyrannis!" In his deranged mind he harbored the absolute conviction that Lincoln was a tyrant, and there were many who agreed with him (as will be seen later in the chapter devoted to Booth).

One of the earliest clear-cut opinions on the matter

was written nearly four centuries before the birth of Christ by the Chinese philosopher Mencius. Like Confucius before him, the great sage believed that emperors ruled by the will of heaven. It had been written in antiquity, "Heaven, having produced the people, appointed for them rulers, and appointed for them teachers, who should be assisting to God."

The problem in Mencius' time was a universal one. All around him he saw corruption and incompetence on the part of the rulers. Perhaps, he thought, the rulers were no longer in favor with heaven, and taking heart from an old proverb which said, "Heaven sees as the people see; heaven hears as the people hear," he concluded that the people must take it upon themselves to determine who possessed the favor of heaven and act upon that knowledge. Thus he wrote that when a monarch ruled contrary to the interests of the people, and was deaf to advice or appeal, it was necessary for that monarch to be removed. The assassination of such a tyrant, wrote Mencius, was not murder, but the will of heaven, for by his actions the tyrant had forfeited his heaven-given right to rule. The philosopher specified three possible approaches: first, that members of the royal house should take it upon themselves to perform the deed; second, that if they could not or would not, some high official should carry out the "removal" with full understanding that he was doing it for the public good rather than for any personal motive; and third, barring the two previous courses, he proposed a "Minister of Heaven," in the person of a popular hero who would rise up from among the masses and raise the standard of righteousness rather than rebellion. Thus, over the long, turbulent course of Chinese history, the people accepted any change of government by assassination, revolt, civil war, or even invasion, as a manifestation of divine will. This millennia-old cultural tradition is even today firmly implanted in the Chinese psyche.

The tradition of tyrannicide in the western world grew along lines parallel to the precepts of Mencius, but in time became hopelessly tangled in complexity.

Among the ancient Greeks there was no equivocation. To begin with, a tyrant was defined not so much as a lawful ruler who abused power, but as a usurper who then abused it. Euripides wrote: "A state has no worse foe than a tyrant, under whom can be no common laws; but one ruler, keeping the law in his own hands, so that equality perishes."

So great was the Greek loathing for tyranny that two of the earliest statues of heroes were in commemoration of the attempt by Harmodius and Aristogeiton to slay the tyrant Hipparchus. This influenced the Athenian historian Xenophon, when he wrote his dialogue on tyranny, and declared of tyrannicides:

> Instead of avenging them, the cities heap honors on the slayer of the despot; and, whereas they exclude the murderer of private persons from the temples, the cities, so far from treating assassins in the same manner, actually put up statues to them in the holy places.[1]

Plato and Aristotle both wrote against tyrants and tyranny, but took no position for or against tyrannicide. Both men, however, took for granted the fact that tyrants invited their own assassination.

It was a lesser known Greek historian, Polybius, who summed up the entire Greek attitude toward tyranny, when he wrote:

It would not be easy to bring a graver or more bitter charge against a man than to call him tyrant, for the mere word, "tyrant" involves the idea of everything that is wickedest, and includes every injustice and crime possible to mankind.

He went on to say:

The killing of a fellow citizen is regarded as a heinous crime, deserving the severest penalties: and yet it is notorious that . . . he who kills a traitor or tyrant in every country receives honors and preeminence.[2]

The Romans, holding dear the concept of the rule of law, were quick to recognize the implications when Julius Caesar named himself dictator for life. Not only did he express his contempt for the constitution, but he defied anyone to challenge his action. Before this the law in respect to dictatorships had been strictly observed: they were permitted only in times of emergency and for limited periods of time. Under the circumstances, many feared that it was only a matter of time before Caesar established a dynastic monarchy. No one took into consideration the fact that Rome had been swept up by events, and that whether Caesar lived or died, the future would not be appreciably altered. Nevertheless, partially motivated by this fear of what Caesar might do, Brutus and Cassius plotted his death.

Although Caesar never had the opportunity to develop into a tyrant, his assassination on the Ides of March in the year 44 B.C. was considered by Cicero to be a preventive measure against tyranny. Alluding to Caesar's death he wrote:

What can be a greater crime than to kill a man, especially one who is an intimate friend? But is he a criminal who has killed a tyrant, even if the tyrant was his friend? It does not seem so to the Roman people, who regard this as the finest of all glorious deeds.[3]

Strong words, these—words that would be quoted again and again over the centuries as a justification for the assassination of anyone considered by the assassins to be a tyrant.

Unfortunately for Rome, the constitution was not restored after Caesar's fall. Though not all the Roman emperors were tyrannical rulers, maniacs like Caligula and Nero most certainly were. Seneca, who was Nero's tutor, must certainly have been thinking of his infamous pupil when he wrote, "No offering is more acceptable to the gods than the blood of a tyrant." And Plutarch, whose lifetime spanned the reigns of Claudius through Hadrian, was most emphatic when expressing his feelings on the subject. Tyrannicide, he said, was a "remarkable act of virtue." Thus, there was ample rationale for future advocates of assassination, many of whom would twist and squeeze the words to suit their own ends.

As Christianity took root, the problems of interpretation increased immensely. St. Paul was most explicit when he wrote in *Romans 13:1-2*, "For there is no power but of God: the powers that be are ordained of God. Whosoever therefore resisteth the power, resisteth the Ordinance of God . . ."

St. Peter was equally specific, saying:

> Submit yourselves to every ordinance of man for the Lord's sake: whether it be to the king, as supreme; or unto governors, as unto them that are sent by him for the punishment of evildoers, and for the praise of them that do well. [*1 Peter 2:13-14*]

Later St. Augustine gave additional weight to the

Christian emphasis on obedience by referring to the Old
Testament. The tyrant, he declared, was certainly "worse
than a beast," but even such a cruel despot as Nero had
"no dominion but from the providence of the great God
who sometimes judges that men deserve such rulers. The
word of God says plainly: 'Through me kings reign, and
tyrants through me hold the earth.'" In paraphrasing
Proverbs 8:15–16 he merely expressed his own affirma-
tion of the concept of rule by divine right.

As time passed, church fathers continued to reinforce
this concept. In the sixth century, Pope Gregory the Great
laid down the principle that offense to a ruler was an
offense against God. There were voices of dissent, however. Two centuries earlier, St. John Chrysostom, a father
of the Greek Church, had interpreted St. Paul's words
to mean that the powers of a ruler's office were ordained
by God, but the ruler himself was not. This provided the
loophole so enthusiastically seized upon by political in-
triguers of the future, less concerned with the distinctions
between "lawful" and "unlawful" rulers than with a
workable rationale for assassination. Isidore of Seville,
a seventh-century church father, widened the loophole even
further when he wrote that kings who did not govern
righteously lost their claim to the title "king." "Kings
are so called by their ruling," he declared. "Therefore,
by doing rightly the title of king is kept, by wrongdoing it
is lost."

Against such a background of conflicting opinion,
medieval assassinations were justified either as having been
committed on behalf of a lawful monarch or against the
person of an unlawful one. Certainly the murder of the
Archbishop of Canterbury, Thomas à Becket, in 1170, was
just such an assassination, the tragedy of which was com-

pounded by the pointlessness of the deed. Despite Becket's
political differences with Henry II, historical evidence
points to the fact that the king never intended to have
the prelate killed. Actually, there was probably no one
in England who regretted his death more. The crime
was committed by four overzealous knights, firmly convinced that they were carrying out the wishes of their
liege, and that their personal fortunes would be enhanced
as a result.

It was during the Renaissance that tyranny and assassination became as commonplace as sunrise and sunset.
Considered by many authorities to represent the prototype
of the tyrant at his worst was Esselino da Romano, who
ruled Padua and Verona in the thirteenth century. "His
ruthless brutality," wrote John D. Lewis in *Against the
Tyrant,* "was to make him the legendary tyrant of Italian
tradition." Murder, torture, kidnapping, and betrayal were
the instruments of his power, and it is said that in Padua
alone he packed eight prisons with his enemies. But none
remained there long, for he kept his executioners working
day and night.

Not all Renaissance Italian tyrants were brutal; some
even won voluntary loyalty from their subjects. All, however, had two things in common: complete ruthlessness
and a thorough lack of ethical restraint. Most, if not all,
subscribed to the Aristotelian theory:

> . . . a tyrant must put on the appearance of religion. Subjects are
> less apprehensive of illegal treatment from a ruler whom they con-
> sider godfearing and pious. On the other hand, they do less easily
> move against him, believing that he has the gods on his side.

Gian Galeazzo Visconti, though remembered for having
built the magnificent cathedral of Milan, was an infamous

despot and the progenitor of heirs even more cruel than himself. One of his sons, Gian Maria, was in the habit of amusing himself by observing his trained dogs tear condemned men to pieces. And of Cesare Borgia so much has been written that it would be redundant to rehash his career at this point.

A superb word-picture of Renaissance tyranny was painted by the historian J.C.L. de Sismondi in 1832, when he wrote:

> Spies watched and denounced every expression of generous feel-ing; they insinuated themselves into families to betray them; they abused the sacred ties of kindred, home and neighborhood, to convert them into snares; they made all feel that the wisdom of the subject consisted in distrusting every one, and not meddling in the affairs of another. Assassination and poisoning were common means of government. Every Italian tyrant was stained with the blood of his kindred; paid murderers dispatched the objects of his suspicions; he outraged public virtue, and could maintain order only by fear. Death itself at length failing to inspire terror, he combined with capital punishment protracted tortures, the ex-hibition of which only rendered men more hardened and fierce. . . . In the fourteenth century it was still worse. . . . Men rose to be princes by crime and perfidy towards their neighbors, and their domestic treachery marked the commencement and duration of every reign. Tyrants were so numerous, so constantly under the observation of every citizen, that their example was always operat-ing to corrupt the people.[4]

Tyrannicide during this period, however, was prompted less by moral principles than by pure political intrigue. There were exceptions—notably the death of Galeazzo Maria Sforza, Duke of Milan, another whose name is a bloody stain on the pages of history. "There was no crime," wrote Sismondi, "of which that false and ferocious man was not believed to be capable." Under his oppres-

sive rule liberty was crushed, and terror became the way
of life. His assassination was a spectacular event, and
was compared by J. D. Symon and S. L. Bensusan, in *The
Renaissance and Its Makers,* to the death of Hipparchus.
Their account of the events leading up to the act itself is
especially worth repeating.

> The end of Galeazzo is not unlike that of the Athenian tyrant
> and the story is equally romantic. It touches very closely the new
> classical spirit that had grown up in the great Italian cities, even
> under the hand of ruthless despots. The Harmodius and Aristo-
> geiton of Milan were two young scholars, Girolamo Olgiati and
> Gian Andrea Lampugnani, both pupils of Nicolo Montano. Their
> study of classical history had made them devout enthusiasts for
> liberty and very good haters of tyranny. To them they joined Carlo
> Visconti, who was of like mind with themselves. His grudge was
> on the score of family usurpation [the duchy of Milan had been
> wrested from the Viscontis by the Sforzas], theirs on the ground
> of family shame, wrought by Galeazzo's profligacy. They resolved
> that the tyrant must die, and went about their project with a cool
> deliberation mingled curiously with a scholarly pose. At the same
> time that they practised the use of the dagger they sought inspiration
> in the pages of Sallust and Tacitus. At length, on the 26th day of
> December, 1476, all was ready.[5]

Since December 26 was St. Stephen's day, the three
young conspirators knew that their victim-to-be would
come to St. Stephen's church to put on a show of piety
for public consumption. They made it a point to arrive
early, in order to offer up a prayer of their own, that had
been specially composed for the occasion by Visconti.
"Fashion Thou our high enterprise," it began, "and be
not wrathful if we must presently stain thine altars with
blood, that so we may free the world of a monster."
When the duke arrived they struck with perfect precision and killed him on the spot. Luckily (for themselves),

Visconti and Lampugnani were quickly slain by Sforza's bodyguards. The hapless Olgiati was taken alive and brutally tortured to death. Notwithstanding this, he refused to repent and maintained to the end that had he to do it again and be tortured tenfold, he would strike the blow without the slightest hesitation. "My death is untimely," he declared. "My fame eternal; the memory of my deed will endure forever."

Unfortunately, on the few occasions like this, when tyrannicide was carried out along classical lines and with idealistic motives, the assassins who survived long enough to witness the aftermath of their deeds learned after the fact what Machiavelli pointed out from observation alone: it was foolish to expect the oppressed masses to rise up against tyranny, even when they were dissatisfied with their lot. And that principle is as valid today as it was then.

But no one paid very much attention to Machiavelli in his time, because if they had, as Professor Giuseppe Prezzolini suggests, he would probably have been burned along with every word he ever wrote. To tyrants, the great political theorist expressed a clear warning: either abandon tyranny altogether, or expect it to backfire. Few chose to abandon it, and fewer still managed to escape a "miserable end."

There was no period of European history in which assassination played a greater role than the turbulent years of the sixteenth century. Political intrigue cloaked itself in the garb of classical tyrannicide again and again. Torn asunder by the bitter hatreds and violent controversies rising out of the Protestant Reformation, enemies, previously at daggers' points over international issues, were driven even further apart by religious differences.

It would require a full volume at the very least to present here a complete picture of the serpentine entanglements and intrigues of that bloody century. We should, however, briefly discuss a few key persons and events that relate specifically to the subject of political murder.

Although, as has already been pointed out, the Protestant Reformation provided a background for the turmoil, leaders of the movement were against assassination of anyone as a political tool. Luther, for all the vicious ravings that spewed from his lips in the twilight of his life, was emphatic in his rejection of the doctrine of tyrannicide, preaching instead traditional obedience to temporal authority. In Geneva, John Calvin warned Admiral Gaspard de Coligny, one of the top leaders of the French Huguenots, to be cautious in resisting persecution by the Catholic power structure. "If a single drop of blood is shed," cautioned the great reformer, "rivers of blood will flow through Europe!" And he was right, but more of that presently.

One of the great ironies of the century arose from the writings of a Spanish Jesuit, Juan de Mariana, who was one of the most able, broadminded thinkers of his time. Historian W. E. H. Lecky said of him:

> The interests of the church, though never forgotten, never eclipse or exclude the interests of the people, and all the barriers that are raised against heresy are equally raised against tyranny.

What all of this amounts to is that Mariana was the chief Catholic advocate of tyrannicide. In his controversial treatise, *De Rege et Regis Institutione,* he maintained the right of a nation to rebel against a tyrannical ruler, regardless of whether he possessed a legitimate title. This was revolutionary thinking in a time when most authorities firmly believed in rule by divine right, especially

when he went on to say that if rebellion were not successful, tyrannicide was proper. Royal power, he asserted, was
derived from the people, who had the right to revoke
it if it was abused. This sounded more like the philosophy
of Mencius than that of a Catholic priest. He based his
arguments in favor of an orderly society on a simple
premise—common need. He wrote:

> At the beginning, men roamed the world like beasts. Inasmuch
> as they saw that their lives were constantly endangered, and also
> that kinsmen abstained from violence and assassination when they
> were united, those who felt oppressed by the powerful started to
> unite. They focused their attention on the one who could be ex-
> pected to prevent all kinds of private and public violence, to
> establish equality, to control affairs by means of laws equally
> applicable to inferiors and superiors. The rulers derived their
> dignity not from intrigues or gifts, but from men of moderation,
> honesty, and other virtues.[6]

The ideal state as conceived by Mariana was free of
tyranny, but his declaration on the disposition of a tyrant
was free of equivocation:

> And if circumstances demand it, if in no other way it is possible
> to save the fatherland, the prince should be killed by the sword
> as a public enemy. . .

He fully recognized that Christian morality would have
to be violated if the state were to be saved by an act of
assassination. This had to be in conflict with his training as
a Jesuit and his credo as a Catholic. But he recognized
that in the final analysis he was a mortal man, and he
said simply, "This is my way of seeing things."
In Venice there lived a contemporary of Mariana, who
advocated assassination as a political expediency, but in
an entirely different frame of reference. His name was
Paolo Sarpi, and though he was a monk, he was more of

a thorn in the seat of the papal throne than he could possibly have been to any Protestant authority. His accomplishments were literary, scientific, and political. But he aroused the ire of the Vatican when he locked horns with Pope Paul V over the matter of church authority in secular affairs. So effective were his tactics, which consisted of pure appeals to reason, that he actually forced the pope to back down, and in the process, he destroyed, or at least seriously undermined, the old conviction that papal excommunications and interdictions were invulnerable.

What Sarpi was really fighting for was a principle that American Revolutionaries were to establish in the eighteenth century—separation of church and state. Though a Catholic himself, he believed that Protestants should be permitted to live in Venice and enjoy the freedom to worship as they chose. Furthermore, he believed and fought for the right of the Venetian republic to oversee its own secular affairs.

It came as a surprise to no one, then, that on a dark night, shortly after his political victory over the Holy See, he was ambushed at the foot of a bridge by a small band of assailants, stabbed, and left for dead. But he survived and made a pun that was to become famous. *"Agnosco stylum Curiae Romanae,"* or, "I recognize the style/dagger of the Roman Curia." (The Latin word *stylum* translates into both "style" and "dagger.") The would-be killers took refuge in one of the papal territories, and the leader claimed that he had been driven to the deed by religious zeal, a shallow alibi indeed for a bankrupt oil merchant.

Sarpi's posthumous treatise on the Republic of Venice specifically recommended the clandestine removal by assassination of citizens who had become too influential for the good of the state, and suggested poison as the best means of dispatching them. He made no apologies for his stand on secret assassination, but rested his theories on strictly political ground. Naturally, his attitude did not serve to illuminate his memory in some quarters, and there were even those who accused him of having ultimately abandoned Christianity itself.

Both Mariana and Sarpi lived during an era when Christians for the most part conducted themselves in a most un-Christian manner. They were influenced by and had influence on the sanguinary events of their time, the bloodiest of which occurred in France during the course of her savage religious wars. Certainly France fell to the very nadir of her history at this time, thereby spawning intrigues, plots, counterplots, and assassinations.

Although the king, Charles IX, physically occupied the throne, his mother, Catherine de Medici, was *de facto* ruler of France. Condemned by some historians as a monster, and praised by others as a strong woman, doing the best she could to keep her adopted country from falling apart at the seams, she is recognized by all as a true product of her Italian Renaissance heritage. "She is still a puzzle after four centuries of conflicting interpretations," wrote Will and Ariel Durant, in *The Age of Reason Begins,* Chapter XIII. "Descended from Lorenzo the Magnificent, grandniece of Pope Leo X, she was a typical Medici, with government in her heritage and subtlety in her blood."

What matters is that her son, a sickly and unstable young man at best, had neither the talent nor the strength of character to rule his own life, let alone a nation in the throes of turmoil. As he fell under the spell of Admiral de Coligny, the Catholic courtiers grew uneasy. The political implications of the king's listening too closely to the most powerful Protestant in France were great. Matters were complicated by the fact that two of the most influential Catholic families, the Guises and the Bourbons, had their eyes on the throne itself.

Catherine, shrewd politician that she was, recognized exactly what was going on and through her private army of spies and informers knew exactly who was poisoning someone here, or planning an assassination there. As long as these intrigues did not interfere with her plans she kept hands off; otherwise she outdid the rest of them. A few cool heads, Catholic and Huguenot alike, urged their respective partisans to live and let live, each to seek salvation his own way. But the majority on both sides refused to listen. In Huguenot strongholds Catholic churches were desecrated, and Catholics mistreated. In predominantly Catholic areas, Protestants were the victims of persecution and repression.

But since real power rested in the hands of the Catholics, they did not hesitate to apply whatever pressure they could against Protestants, not only for religious reasons, but for political ones as well. The Protestants, unwilling to be converted, banished, or wiped out, fought back as hard as they could. Armies were raised, battles were fought, and people died crying, "God is on our side!"

In this atmosphere of political hatred, religious persecution, political intrigue, poisoning, stabbing, and civil war, by the summer of 1572 France was on the brink of disintegration. No one was more aware of the situation than Catherine de Medici. Furthermore, there was the additional threat of foreign enemies taking advantage of this terrible disunity, and swooping down on the demoralized French like hungry vultures. It occurred to her that she might succeed in unifying the Catholics and Protestants by marrying her daughter, Marguerite of Valois, to the popular Protestant, King Henry of Navarre. Despite the seemingly insurmountable obstacles to such a union, all parties involved agreed reluctantly to compromises and the wedding day was set. There remained, however, one thorn in Catherine's side—Admiral de Coligny. He took advantage of the king's confidence in him by urging the young sovereign to wage war against Spain and aid the neighboring Dutch to throw off the oppressive yoke of Spanish rule. Among other things, this could effectively strengthen Protestant influence in Europe. The adverse implications from the Catholic viewpoint were enormous.

There was only one way to deal with this threat once and for all. Coligny had to go! Catherine, prompted by dire warnings of a Huguenot conspiracy against the royal family, ordered the assassination of the admiral.

In all fairness to the illustrious Huguenot, it should be remembered that he was a Frenchman first, and probably his prime motive for advising war against an external enemy was to unify Catholic and Protestant elements into a cohesive nation again. This political gambit has been used successfully by leaders of all nations.

The powerful House of Guise had a special grudge against Coligny. Nine years earlier, the Duke of Guise had been ambushed and assassinated by a hotheaded young Huguenot, who had implicated the admiral. Although he had admitted knowing the youth, and giving him money, he swore that he had been in no way connected with the Duke's murder, and the charge was never proven. Yes, Coligny's death would please the Guises immensely—especially the dowager duchess, who burned with a desire to see her husband avenged.

Thus, on the night of August 22, two shots rang out while Coligny was walking home from the Louvre, and he fell, bleeding, to the pavement. The king was furious when he heard the news and sent his personal physician to attend his wounded adviser. Word of the attempted assassination spread like a brushfire through Paris, and the Huguenots were infuriated. Some of Coligny's aides, suspecting the hand of the Guises, were all for immediate retaliation, but the admiral would not permit such a move. Nevertheless, sullen crowds of Huguenots milled about the Louvre and threatened to take the law into their own hands if the bungling assassins were not apprehended and brought to justice. Others gathered about the Hôtel de Lorraine, where the Guises were housed, and shouted curses and death threats.

By the night of the 23rd, tempers were so high and nerves so taut that all of Paris was like a keg of powder with a short, sizzling fuse.

Catherine and her advisers were convinced that Coligny and the five principal Huguenot leaders had to be assassinated, but the act could not be carried out unless the king gave his permission. He was on the verge of nervous collapse, but he refused to be party to such cold-blooded murder. His mother and her counsellors harangued him, insisting that if the multiple assassinations were not carried out immediately, a huge army of Huguenots would seize Paris, kidnap the royal family, and heaven knows what else. Finally, worn down by their continuous bleating, Charles clapped his hands to his ears in a fit of rage and frustration, cursing them as he gave in, but adding, "If you must kill the admiral, then so be it! But if that is the case, then you will have to kill every Huguenot in France, so none will remain to cast the finger of reproach at me!"

Thus, what began as a hasty plan to assassinate six persons degenerated into a wanton scheme to commit deliberate genocide—all because of the thoughtless and ill-timed remark of a weak young man whose word could be interpreted as law. The edict was then hurriedly drawn up, plans were made to carry out the slaughter, and as the hands of the clock moved relentlessly forward, the specter of a nightmare assumed the flesh and bones of reality.

Admiral de Coligny was the first to be murdered under the supervision of the Guises who had yearned so long for his death. At the end of St. Bartholomew's Day, the streets of Paris ran red with Protestant blood and were littered with their corpses. But it did not end there. In an orgy of violence, the citizens of Paris joined eagerly in the spirit of the massacre, and for the next two days Protestants were dragged from their homes to be shot, stabbed, burned, and clubbed to death. No mercy was shown. Men, women, children, regardless of age or social standing, were ruthlessly hunted down and slain. A few prominent Protestants, including Henry of Navarre, were spared by order of the queen mother, but the mass butchery, completely out of hand, went on until September 17 in Paris, and until October 3 in the provinces. It is estimated that approximately 10,000 perished in Paris alone, and as many as 50,000 died altogether.

The Protestant nations were sickened and shocked. Queen Elizabeth of England donned mourning to receive the French Ambassador. The Kirk of Scotland called for a retaliatory massacre of Catholics in that country, but fortunately reason prevailed. Although Pope Gregory XIII ordered masses of thanksgiving to be celebrated, bonfires to be lit, and a commemorative medal to be struck in honor of the massacre, not all Catholics rejoiced. There were too many of them who knew what it was like to be on the receiving end. Unfortunately, history records more about those who did rejoice, like the pope and Philip II of Spain, who is reported to have laughed on hearing the news, proclaiming the event one of the most memorable triumphs in the history of Christianity.

To many it seemed as though Protestantism had received its death blow. Nothing, however, could have been further from the truth. There seems to be a natural law in effect which always strengthens persecuted peoples, so that the greater the persecution, the stronger they become. There is only one way to effectively wipe out a people, and that is to absorb them. In any event, adverse reaction died down as rapidly then as it does today in the wake of a massacre. Circumstances may change, but human nature remains constant. In the long run, therefore, all the St. Bartholomew's Day Massacre accomplished was to intensify hatred, promote more intrigue, and guarantee future bloodshed. Inevitably, Protestants were granted the right to worship as they chose, and when Charles IX died, his lungs eaten away by tuberculosis, and his mind by remorse, he was only twenty-three. Indeed, his epitaph might well have carried a warning for future generations not to trust kings under thirty.

The young monarch's death actually strengthened his mother's hold on the reins of government. His brother, the former Duke of Anjou, having been shoved reluctantly onto the throne of Poland, fled his chilly domain to don the crown of France with an angry horde of Polish subjects at his heels, furious at this royal abandonment. As Henry III he promised to continue the official policy of Huguenot persecution. The Protestants were told either to embrace Catholicism or leave the country. But since the new king seemed more given to threats than to action, they stiffened their political resistance and continued to fight for religious freedom at home. They, too, were Frenchmen, and they had no intention of changing their nationality without a struggle.

In time, however, Henry III became more profligate in his ways and proved to be no improvement over his late brother.

In the face of rising Protestant influence, a political party calling itself the Catholic League formed under the banner of the Guises. They had powerful foreign allies, notably the pope and Philip II of Spain. Although the religious aspect of the matter was an important factor, there is no question that beneath it all the Duke of Guise was planning to maneuver himself onto the throne of France. The king and his immediate circle could not help but be aware of the situation. The country was fragmented and flying apart at the seams again, thanks to civil war, foreign and domestic intrigues reaching into every part of the land, and no real leadership.

By 1588 the situation had become so grave that the populace of Paris rose up in revolt and besieged the king at the Louvre. The Catholic League boldly set up a revolutionary government and began negotiating with Spain to invade France, thereby assisting in the establishment of a strong Catholic regime which would take a firm, no-nonsense attitude toward Protestantism. Philip II was delighted with the idea because it fit in perfectly with his own plans. He had determined to avenge the execution of Catholic Mary, Queen of Scots, by Protestant Elizabeth the First. It was an ideal excuse to launch the mighty Spanish armada against England, assist his Catholic allies in France, and assert Spanish power as never before. Besides, he had one eye on the fabulous resources of the New World and the time for him to make a decisive power grab was at hand.

Everything seemed to go against Henry III. He was forced to flee to Chartres, and his end appeared imminent. Though his enemies would not go so far as to depose

him, they had the upper hand. He was forced by them
to proscribe Protestantism. But then, events overtook men,
as is so often the case, and the British sank Spanish
dreams along with the armada, shattering Philip's
grandiose plans. Henry, taking heart from his adversaries'
crushing defeat, decided to strike a blow of his own.
Without bothering to weigh the consequences he ordered
the assassination of the Duke of Guise and his brother,
the Cardinal of Guise.

The murders were carried out just two days before
Christmas in 1588, and when Henry triumphantly revealed
to his mother what he had done, she was horrified.
Recognizing the assassinations as rash and stupid, she
saw as the only outcome the collapse of the House of
Valois. In less than two weeks she died a broken and
unlamented woman.

With his characteristic lack of perceptivity, Henry cried,
"Now I am the king!" But what was he king of? On one
side the Catholic League was in open revolt. On the
other angry Huguenots, their patience exhausted, loudly
demanded his deposal, arguing that he was a tyrant. He
was caught between two onrushing forces that were
rapidly closing in on him. In Paris students took to the
streets and demonstrated for the king's overthrow. Everywhere priests called for violent revolution, and all over
France skirmishing—both verbal and physical—erupted
explosively. The situation was worse than ever.

Recognizing deteriorating conditions as an ideal spring-
board from which to make a fresh bid for power, Protestant Henry of Navarre volunteered to stand by the king
in his time of need. This only served to unhinge Catholic
extremists to the point of no return. Once again the fuse
sputtered dangerously near the magazine, and on August 1,

1589, a naïve Dominican monk, Jacques Clément, having been brainwashed by firebrands, took up the assassin's dagger and fatally stabbed Henry in the abdomen. The poor fool was thoroughly convinced that he had performed an act of licit tyrannicide. But all he accomplished was to ensure the accession of a Protestant to the throne. For, while breathing his last, the dying sovereign named his cousin Henry of Navarre to succeed him.

The fourth Henry to sit on the throne of France, Henry of Navarre was the first Bourbon. Like his immediate predecessors, he was crowned amid chaos, but unlike them he proved to be strong, determined, and capable. Although it took him years to unify the country, he succeeded by means of military and political moves, all of which were well chosen and proved successful. His conversion to Catholicism in July 1593 was one of his shrewdest political moves. Eventually he became immensely popular, and earned the title Henry the Great, yet, despite his achievements, he was constantly the target of fanatical would-be assassins. Perhaps, had he not been endowed with such reckless courage, he might have died of old age. Unfortunately, such was not his destiny. On May 14, 1610, while riding in the royal carriage on his way to visit his trusted adviser, the Duke of Sully, Henry IV was stabbed to death by a religious fanatic named François Ravaillac. It was the irony of ironies. Ravaillac, tormented by fantasies that the king was going to launch a war against the Vatican, and after digesting inflammatory pamphlets on tyrannicide, struck down one of the few kings in history least deserving such a death. But as he was torn to pieces by a vengeful, bloodthirsty Parisian mob, Ravaillac, like assassins before him and many to come, died fully believing that he had slain a tyrant.

3

THE IMPACT of the ASSASSIN on HISTORY

Although, as events of the sixteenth century amply demonstrated, assassins played a prominent part in the tumultuous struggles between nations and between ideologies, not all assassinations have had a profound effect on history. Yet, throughout the ages certain momentous assassinations had a tremendous influence on the future and, upon occasion, so did attempts that failed. Historical fact notwithstanding, there have been those, like Benjamin Disraeli, one of England's great prime ministers, who believed otherwise. After the death of Abraham Lincoln he remarked, "Assassination has never changed the history of the world."

How, then, can we determine what constitutes a high-impact assassination? To such a question we can only pose another question: "How many lives might have been saved if the assassination plot of July 20, 1944 against Adolf Hitler had succeeded?" One of the plans of the conspirators was to end the European phase of World War II by asking the Allies for peace once the Nazi government was effectively overthrown. Admittedly it is difficult to make absolute statements as to what might or might not have happened as the result of the death or survival of an important political figure. It is not difficult, however, to make educated guesses on the basis of historical fact. And since this is an era of violence and assassination, all one needs to do is look around, pay close attention to what is happening, and draw the appropriate conclusions.

Since it is impossible to discuss every historically significant assassination in sufficient detail to do each one justice, the next best thing is to do justice to those that are discussed. Probably the earliest assassination with any far-reaching consequences was that of Philip II of Macedon in the year 336 B.C. As master of Greece, he hatched grandiose plans for the conquest of Asia, and was unquestionably one of the most powerful men of his time, with an illustrious future before him. However, like so many other great men before and after him, his domestic life was far from idyllic.

After fathering a string of illegitimate children, he divorced his wife, Olympias, accusing her of infidelity, and then promptly selected a new bride. This humiliated the cast-off queen and enraged Alexander, her son. Not only was this an insult to his mother, but it cast a shadow over his own legitimacy, thereby raising a serious doubt that he would ever succeed his father. The prince's fears were reinforced at Philip's subsequent marriage feast when he overheard one of his father's drunken generals say flippantly that he hoped the new queen would produce a lawful heir to the kingdom of Macedonia. Infuriated by this slur, Alexander hurled a full cup of wine at the general's head, and cried, "You dare to call me a bastard, you swine!" At which Philip jumped up, drew his sword, and would have slain his son on the spot had he not been too drunk to navigate the short distance between them. As he clattered to the floor, Alexander sneered and declared, "Behold the great man who is preparing to lead an army into Asia, and who falls to the ground like a helpless child!"

After this touchy incident, Alexander and his mother, Olympias, prudently departed from Philip's capital. Later, in order to cement shaky political relations, Philip arranged for Alexander's sister to marry her uncle, the brother of Olympias. A magnificent celebration was staged for the occasion, including athletic games, colorful processions, and other lavish public entertainments, and the marriage was treated as a national holiday.

Crowning the festivities was a theatrical spectacular written and staged especially for the occasion, to which Philip had invited all of his distinguished guests, including delegates from abroad. After his entire entourage was seated in the amphitheater he prepared to make his grand entrance. Trumpets blared and a hush fell over the crowd as all heads turned toward the royal portal. Suddenly a stranger sprang from the shadows of a darkened passageway. With a single, mighty lunge, he thrust a gleaming short sword into the startled Philip's body, then whirled about and dashed in the direction of a waiting horse outside. The action was so swift, so daring, and so well timed, that the assassin had every chance of escaping unharmed had it not been for a quirk of fate. As he fled from the scene of the crime with the royal bodyguards hard on his heels like a pack of enraged hunting dogs, he caught his sandal on a vinestock and stumbled, helpless, to the ground. In a flash the guards were upon him, shouting, cursing, stabbing, and slashing. When they had done, he had been torn to pieces.

It has been suggested that the queen mother, Olympias, was the hand behind the hand of Pausanius, the assassin. Whether she was or not, the deed permitted Alexander to ascend the throne of Macedon and carve out an empire. For had his father lived, and named as lawful heir the infant son of his second wife, the career of Alexander the Great would never have been launched.

The next significant assassination in the ancient world took place about two hundred years later in Rome. It may not have had an appreciable affect on the course of history, but it is worth mentioning here because the main issue involved—agrarian reform—is not an unfamiliar problem in the modern world, and it demonstrates that today's struggles are not so different from those of the past. The victim was Tiberius Gracchus, a Roman patrician and tribune. Rich landowners controlled vast estates manned by slave labor, while poor, free Roman farmers, possessing meager plots of land, could barely eke out a living. Gracchus had an illustrious heritage. His father was Sempronius Gracchus, a distinguished Roman tribune, and his mother, Cornelia, was renowned as daughter of Cornelius Scipio Africanus, the general who had defeated Hannibal. But, though very much a part of the Establishment, Tiberius and his brother Gaius were radicals, favoring revolutionary changes unfavorable to the Establishment. They were primarily after agrarian land reform which would redistribute the farm land more equitably. The idea was not as radical as it seemed on the surface because, technically, the wealthy property holders who owned tens of thousands of acres were violating the so-called Licenian Law, which limited any one citizen to the possession of five hundred acres of land.

In his official capacity as tribune, Tiberius succeeded in

pushing through an agrarian reform bill that would not
just enforce the old law, but would actually result in land
redistribution. The wealthy landholding senators were
infuriated, and the patricians in general accused Tiberius
of being a traitor to his class. But when, contrary to law,
he tried to get himself elected to a second term as tribune,
a riot ensued and, in the words of Francis Johnson:

> The senators, who were armed with clubs, canes, stones, or
> whatever weapon they could lay their hands on, rushed upon
> the crowd of voters, overthrew, beat, and killed them, stamping
> them under their feet and quickly and irresistibly advancing to-
> ward the spot where they beheld the man who was the object of
> their rage and bloodthirstiness. Tiberius, unarmed and forsaken
> by his friends, turned round to seek safety in flight, but, stumbling
> over those who had been knocked down, fell to the ground. It
> was at that moment, while Tiberius was trying to get on his feet
> again, that one of his own colleagues, a tribune of the people,
> dealt him a powerful and fatal blow, striking him on the head
> with the leg of a stool. Others rushed up and struck him again
> and again, but it was only a lifeless corpse which suffered from
> their abuse. Three hundred of his friends had fallen with him. It
> was the first Roman blood which had been shed in civil war, and
> this first conflict deprived Rome of one of its most illustrious
> citizens.[1]

Gaius Gracchus carried on his brother's work, but unfortunately the opposition was too strong for him, too,
and he was forced to commit suicide twelve years later.

The assassination of Julius Caesar is probably the most
celebrated political murder in history. Yet, when we look
at subsequent Roman history, it is safe to say that had
Caesar lived to become the first emperor of Rome, the
general sequence of events would not have been greatly
altered. In all probability the chaos and civil war that

raged until Augustus donned the imperial robes would not have occurred. But it is most likely that the most significant single outgrowth of Caesar's assassination was the rationale it provided for future political assassins.

In distinct contrast to the death of Caesar is the assassination in 656 A.D. of Caliph Othman, whose murder marked the first blood shed by a Moslem at the hands of another Moslem, and paved the way for an unbroken tradition of violence and assassination in the Middle East from that time on. Imagine what might have been had the word of Mohammed been strictly obeyed, and no Moslem ever stained the earth with the blood of a fellow believer. Certainly the entire history of Islam would have been vastly different and, consequently, the entire course of world history.

Sometimes, though, an assassination has had little political consequence in the long run, despite the tremendous effect it had in other ways. Like the death of Julius Caesar, the murder of Macbeth by Scottish King Malcolm III, in the year 1057, inspired William Shakespeare to write one of his best-known plays. There is hardly a person who can read, anywhere in the world, who does not know the story of Macbeth. So, in a sense, though the power struggle between these two relatively minor medieval figures was of small consequence in the overall fabric of world events, it was engraved indelibly on the pages of history because a single literary genius, fascinated by the universality of its drama, gave it immortality.

The historical significance of events great and small is

often diminished by the passage of time, the effect being
almost like looking at something through the wrong end
of a telescope. Thus, the farther removed we are from
any atrocity of the past, the less emotional our reaction
to it. One of our basic human flaws is the ability to
calmly read about the savage slaughters of Ivan the Terrible, yet boil over with outrage when we learn of some
contemporary barbarity, which, when stripped of its emotional overtones, is far less malefic by comparison. It was
this characteristic that permitted Nikolai Mikhailovitch
Karamzin, the great Russian historian, to write glowingly
of Ivan, despite the fact that he was universally regarded
as a monster.

> Such was the Czar! Such were his subjects! Their patience
> was boundless, for they regarded the commands of the Czar as
> the commands of God, and they considered every act of dis-
> obedience to the Czar's will as a rebellion against the will of God.
> They perished, but they saved for us, the Russians of the 19th
> century, the greatness and the power of Russia, for the strength
> of an empire rests in the willingness of an empire to obey.[2]

As the contemporary British writer Ronald Seth commented in his book *The Executioners,* the harsh autocracy
of Ivan and his successors was probably the only thing
that could possibly have held the diverse ethnic groups of
Russia together as a nation.

Fortunately, as far as Western Europe was concerned,
Ivan the Terrible was more interested in trade than war.
He acquired Asian territories, but lost western ones in
the course of his disastrous European adventures. The
mark he left on the Russian psyche, however, is felt to
this day. Despite their rejection of the old imperialism
(at least in name), post-revolutionary Russians never

hesitated for a moment to glorify those aspects of it which tended to reinforce their own politics. Consequently, after the bloody Stalinist purges of the 1930's, the sixteenth-century czar was significantly rehabilitated. In the epic cinema *Ivan the Terrible,* the czar's ruthless extermination of the boyars who opposed him was depicted as having been for the good of the Russian people. The parallel between Ivan's massacres and Stalin's purges was not lost on those with any degree of perceptivity, especially since the actor portraying Ivan's principal enemy bore a striking resemblance to Stalin's arch foe, Leon Trotsky, who was assassinated in Mexico in 1940 by an agent of SMERSH—a real organization made known by the fictional exploits of James Bond, which will be discussed in Chapter 4.

Although the reign of Ivan the Terrible was marked by a seemingly endless orgy of bloodshed and cruelties, this czar did not ascend the throne of Russia unlawfully. He developed into the wholesale assassin gradually, eventually becoming the first Russian ruler to assume the title "Czar of all the Russias," and thanks to the "patience" mentioned by Karamzin, managed to live out his life and die of natural causes.

It was another Russian sovereign, ultimately to be called "The Great," who reached the throne via intrigues, elaborate plots, and eventually assassination—Catherine the Second. Born Sophia Augusta, Princess of Anhalt-Zerbst, she was the very model of female Prussian nobility, possessing great beauty, intelligence, and charm. She was married in 1745 to a young German prince, Peter, son of Charles Frederick, Duke of Holstein-Gottorp and Grand Duchess Anna of Russia. Peter, who had been groomed for the throne of Denmark and Sweden, was

designated by his childless aunt, the Empress Elizabeth
of Russia, as her heir. She tried her best to transform
him into a Russian, but to no avail.

> He remained not only at heart, but also in his tastes, his man-
> nerisms, his conduct, his amusements and occupations a German;
> and what was worse, he liked to show publicly and privately how
> strongly attached he was to the land of his birth, and how pro-
> foundly he despised the people of Russia, over whom he was to
> rule.[3]

After being baptized in the Orthodox Church, Sophia
Augusta took the name Catherine and, by 1762, when her
husband became Czar Peter III of Russia, the two hated
each other with a passion that could truly be deemed
royal. But there were political as well as personal reasons
for the wedge between them. The new czar alienated his
most influential nobles and virtually his entire army in
one fatal swoop by trying to remake Russia in the image
of his ideal, the Kingdom of Prussia. He made matters
worse by withdrawing from the traditional Franco-Austrian
alliance. Catherine—whose political genius has been compared by historians to that of Elizabeth I of England—had
a burning ambition to be Empress of Russia in her own
right, and was quick to act upon the opportunities presented to her.

Peter III pushed through reforms he naïvely believed
would transform him into the ideal "benevolent despot,"
but which only made more enemies among the nobility,
the top hierarchy of the Church, and the army. Catherine,
acting upon his mistakes like a consummate chess player,
and with boundless skill, soon had succeeded in securing
the loyalty of key figures in all three of these powerful
groups. A clue to her success can be obtained directly
from her memoirs, in which she candidly admitted:

If I may venture to be frank, I would say about myself that I
was every inch a gentleman with a mind much more male than
female; but together with this I was anything but masculine and
combined with the mind and temperament of a man, the attractions of a lovable woman . . .[4]

As tension between Catherine and her husband increased, her position became tenuous at best. The czar
had branded her son, Paul, a bastard, and threatened to
divorce her and marry his mistress. Worse yet, rumors
that she was planning to stage a *coup d'état* leaked out,
thereby forcing her hand. Warned of the leak late on the
night of June 28, 1762, she had no choice but to take the
bold step which would win her an empire or cost her her
head. After dressing hastily she slipped from Peterhof, her
residence, and, under cover of darkness, drove by coach
to St. Petersburg, the capital, arriving just before dawn. At
seven A.M., mounted astride a magnificent stallion and
clad in the resplendent uniform of an Imperial Guards
general, she headed for the armory of the Preobrazhenzky
Guards. Accompanying Catherine were her two favorite
lovers, the handsome and dashing counts Gregor and
Alexis Orloff, who led an escort of other loyal guard
officers.

Earlier, the soldiers at the armory had been prepared
for the events to come by another conspirator, Princess
Catherina Dashkova, who told them that the czar had
suddenly died, and that the Empress Catherine would soon
appear to receive their oaths of allegiance. The three regi-
ments stationed there received the news with wild enthusiasm, and when the beautiful Catherine arrived, she was
greeted with shouts and cheers. The oaths of allegiance
were freely given. Next the party proceeded to the Church
of Kazan, where the entire clergy of St. Petersburg had

gathered, in whose presence the Archbishop of Novgorod administered the oath of imperial office. After a solemn Te Deum, cannon roared, and the multitudes who had gathered loudly rejoiced, for Russia had a new ruler.

There was a slight catch, however. Peter III still lived. He had no idea of what had occurred, for he was away with his mistress at Oranienbaum, the imperial summer retreat, about twenty miles from the capital. He found out soon enough and, had he heeded the advice of his remaining loyal generals, he might very well have reversed the tide, crushed the *coup d'état,* and consolidated his grip on the throne once and for all. But he vacillated, first issuing one order, then rescinding it in favor of another. All around him were confusion and consternation. His advisers urged him to act decisively, while his mistress and her lady friends wept and wrung their hands. During this period of indecision Catherine tightened her own power.

Historians differ as to whether or not Catherine was directly responsible for her husband's assassination. His inherent weakness showed itself when he readily displayed willingness to retire with a pension. Whatever may have gone on in Catherine's mind, it is known that on July 17, just eighteen days after the coup, Alexis Orloff, accompanied by four other officers, and bearing an order from the empress authorizing their admission, visited the deposed czar in his apartment at Oranienbaum, where he was being held under arrest. On the pretense of coming to dine with him, the officers gave Peter a bottle of poisoned wine, but it wasn't quite strong enough to finish him off. With a grimace and a shout, he clutched his throat in agony and leaped to his feet screaming that he had been poisoned. The scene erupted into a melee.

The table was overturned, and china and crystal shattered into splinters on the floor as Orloff and his four accomplices struggled to bring down the czar, cursing, shouting, and knocking over chairs. Peter was a huge man, and he fought with the desperation of a cornered beast, but the five others were too much for him. When the dust had cleared away, he lay dead, strangled by a napkin.

Now only one minor threat to Catherine's position remained. The former czar, Ivan VI, had been deposed as an infant by the late empress, Elizabeth, Peter's predecessor. Imprisoned as a child in the Schlusselburg fortress, he was still alive, a half-mad vegetable of a creature. While he lived there was always the possibility that he might be released by opportunists and used by them as the instrument of Catherine's overthrow, after which he could be placed on the throne as a puppet with an aura of legitimacy about him. Anticipation of such a move had resulted in his jailors receiving strict orders to kill him should anyone ever attempt to effect his release. He ceased to be a threat in the year 1764 when the orders were carried out and he was granted the final release of death.

Catherine the Great died in 1796 after a glorious reign of thirty-four years. Her influence on Russia was tremendous, for she had much to do with westernizing the country, continuing what had been initiated by Peter the Great at the beginning of the century. What direction Russia might have taken without her is hard to say. Certainly she bore great responsibility for an expansionist foreign policy toward the West.

Unquestionably the most dramatic assassination of the eighteenth century occurred in Paris just three years be-

fore the death of Catherine the Great. It was the eve of
the infamous Reign of Terror, and the victim, Jean Paul
Marat, was the rabble-rousing journalist whose incendiary
writings had incited mob violence, riots, and murder. His
assassin, a beautiful girl from Normandy, Charlotte
Corday, was unshakably convinced that if she did not
destroy this "monster," as she referred to him, France
would be thrown into even greater chaos than it was
already engulfed in.

Her genteel appearance and physical beauty were sufficient to fool Marat completely and, over the objections
of his wife and sister, he received Charlotte, believing
that she would provide him with the names of political
enemies from her native town of Caen. He was not dis-
appointed at first, for she did exactly that. But as Marat
triumphantly promised that each of them would soon
lose his head to Madame Guillotine, Charlotte reached
into the folds of her dress, drew out an ebony-handled
kitchen knife, and plunged its gleaming six-inch blade
into the firebrand's chest. Thus died the man who had
recently cried out that in order to ensure public tranquillity two hundred thousand heads should be chopped off.

Unfortunately Charlotte Corday's rash act did not save
France, did not stave off the Terror, and served only to
cost her her own lovely head. Yet because of her youth,
her beauty, and the unquestioned altruism of her motives, she has gone down in history as a tragic heroine
rather than as a hardened murderess. But more important,
she must be remembered as a symbol of the futility
that is so often the result of impetuousness, despite the
fact that she had been planning to kill Marat for some
time before she committed the deed. By allowing her
judgment to be overcome by her emotion, she failed to
foresee that even by stilling Marat's vicious voice and

pen, she could accomplish little more than her own martyrdom.

It would not be difficult to fill an entire volume with only the assassinations of the nineteenth century, beginning with the murder of Czar Paul I in 1801 by a group of dissenting nobles. It was almost a carbon copy of the death of his father, Peter III, but in a sense that explains the crime, for the conspirators were afraid that Paul was indeed a carbon copy of his father—a Prussian, who despised them. The attitude of the Russian military clique was significantly expressed shortly after the czar's death at a dinner party, when Count Münster, the Prussian ambassador to St. Petersburg, stated his disapproval of the deed.

"My dear count," said one of the officers, in defense of the conspirators, "you shouldn't blame us for defending ourselves. Our Magna Charta is tyranny, or if you prefer to call it so, absolutism, tempered by assassination, and our rulers should regulate their conduct accordingly."[5]

Few can argue, despite Disraeli, that the assassination of Abraham Lincoln did not change the entire course of American history. (See Chapter 6.) Had he lived there might have been a policy of true conciliation toward the defeated ex-confederacy instead of one bent on exacting vengeance, destined to create an emotional schism in America that has never been entirely mended.

While Americans, inured to violence by the recent Civil War, settled down to violently winning their own West, Europeans—especially Eastern Europeans—began toying with revolutionary new ideas. Karl Marx had already begun to make his influence felt and, in Russia, certain liberal reforms of Czar Alexander II began backfiring under the most ironic of circumstances. His father,

Nicholas I, had been an absolute dictator, whose rigid censorship and oppressive secret police ensured the maintenance of his xenophobic policies.

Alexander's reforms, however, were not received with the universal acclaim he had hoped for. To be sure, many of his subjects were able to breathe more easily without the constant fear of arrest or harassment by the secret police. The serfs, now suddenly emancipated from centuries of slavery, were unable to cope with a way of life they did not understand, never having been prepared for it. Furthermore, in the atmosphere of greater freedom, extremists overreacted by launching campaigns of terrorism that were to reverberate around the world.

One group, the Nihilists, advocated the total destruction of society as it existed—government, church, and all other social institutions. Their alibi was that universal corruption and despotism had to be wiped out once and for all, and at any cost. They had no reforms in mind, which, of course, was their most glaring mistake. Toppling the Establishment was one thing, but to pull it down with the vague hope that future generations would somehow manage to reconstruct something better out of the wreckage was myopic and downright stupid.

A series of assassinations and assassination attempts on various high-level officials only served to erase from the mind of Alexander II any ideas he might have had about instituting more reforms. Quite to the contrary, there was increased repression against revolutionaries, liberals, and others advocating radical change, all of which only strengthened the resolve of the opposing sides. The principal result of this mutual antagonism was an increase of terrorism, fear, and counterreaction. The czar himself had a number of close brushes with death at the hands of would-be assassins, but his luck abandoned him on

March 13, 1881 (a scant four months before the assassination of United States President James A. Garfield).

Shortly before noon, while Alexander was riding in the imperial carriage to the Winter Palace at St. Petersburg, along the bank of the St. Michael's Canal, a man darted out of the crowd and hurled a dynamite bomb, which exploded, killing two guards and wounding three others. As the horses snorted, whinnied, and reared in terror, the door to the carriage flew open and the czar jumped to the pavement, exclaiming loudly, "Thank God I wasn't hurt!" To which the bomber, who was being dragged away, cried out, "Perhaps you've thanked God too soon!" Suddenly, another bomb flew through the air, landing this time at the czar's feet. So violent was the force of the explosion that windows on the other side of the canal were shattered, a number of people were killed and wounded, and the Romanoff least deserving of such a cruel end, horribly mutilated by the blast, died in agony within the hour. The battle lines were now irrevocably drawn for the long struggle leading to the Revolution of 1917, and the final eclipse of the Romanoff dynasty.

The political murder that had, up to this point, the most immediate, cataclysmic results was the assassination of the heir to the throne of the Austro-Hungarian Empire, Archduke Franz Ferdinand, and his morganatic wife, Sophie, on June 28, 1914. The story of the crime itself has been told so often and in such detail that there is no need to elaborate on it here. The staggering repercussions of the events of that day in the dusty little Bosnian village of Sarajevo are what concern us most. All of Europe was poised on the brink of war, yet, paradoxically, hesitant to make any warlike moves. Admittedly this is oversimplification, but those were the days when heads of state still felt it necessary to observe the time-honored tradition of declaring war before firing a shot or sending troops across a frontier. Consequently the situation was dangerously flammable, the slightest spark would set off an explosion, and no one wanted to be responsible for igniting it. Otto von Bismarck, Germany's "Iron Chancellor," shrewd politician that he was, had prophetically called the shots before the turn of the century, when he said that "some damn fool thing in the Balkans" would trigger the next war.

What no one had counted on was the monumental irony of the incident destined to shatter the peace of the world as it had never been shattered before. The Austro-Hungarian Empire was in such a state of decline that it could not have survived much longer under any circumstances. Therefore, had he lived, Franz Ferdinand would have inherited a paper throne, and political unrest among Serbian extremists was bound to boil over sooner or later. They resented Austrian domination, and it was only a matter of time before someone committed an act of violent protest. The Balkans were the traditional hotspot of Europe. Nevertheless, it is quite conceivable that a different act of terrorism might have had a more localized impact, and less far-reaching consequences. There is a theory that certain high-level Austrians, eager for war, had engaged in some risky, behind-the-scenes maneuvering, to place the none-too-popular Franz Ferdinand in a vulnerable position that might prove provocative enough to invite his assassination. Whether this is so or not, it is so that the course of history was abruptly altered when the sixteen Serbian conspirators, led by Gavrilo Princip, had concluded their daring assault.

Edmund Taylor, in *The Fall of Dynasties,* wrote:

Not only did he fire the shots himself, but—though he was only a nineteen-year-old high school student at the time—he was the moral leader of the assassination conspiracy and its field commander. He is not just a Balkan folk hero but a twentieth-century one; by his act he ushered in a whole age of conspiracy, a time of assassins.[6]

But, significant as the assassination at Sarajevo was, insofar as it served as the detonator for the actual outbreak of World War I, it did not *cause* the war.

There were approximately 160 assassinations and assassination attempts throughout the world in the period between the end of the First World War and the kidnapping on June 10, 1924 of Giacomo Matteotti. As secretary of the Socialist Party in Italy and an influential member of the Chamber of Deputies, Matteotti was one of Fascism's most outspoken enemies.

While others held their tongues in the face of Mussolini's increasing imposition of fascist terror, Matteotti dared to warn the Italian people what lay in store for them if they permitted a fascist party to attain absolute power. To Mussolini, then, Matteotti represented a serious threat, for if the courageous deputy were not silenced, Il Duce might remain only the leader of his own party, and never achieve the power he sought. The eyes of the world were on Italy—especially those of one of Mussolini's most ardent admirers, a relatively obscure Austrian malcontent named Adolf Hitler.

When Matteotti disappeared, it seemed at first as though his kidnapping would prove to be the downfall of the fascist party, for Italians were outraged at this act of blatant gangsterism against the person of an extremely popular public figure. Anti-fascist sentiment rose even higher when Matteotti's remains were discovered in a shallow grave in a forest outside Rome, and it was learned that he had been murdered. In fact, it could be said that at this point Fascism reached its all-time low watermark. But here fate stepped in, dealing Italy, and indeed the whole world, a cruel blow. Mussolini and his cohorts, realizing that they had reached the crucial point of their political lives as a result of this crisis, threw caution to the winds and gambled that they might succeed in pushing through oppressive laws which would guarantee them control of Italy before public opinion strengthened their opposition and put the fascist party out of business. The move worked. But though he won for himself a brief moment of glory, Benito Mussolini only succeeded in bringing ultimate misery to Italy. Instead of forging a twentieth-century Roman Empire, he spawned a nightmare that would eventually lead him to an ignominious death at the hands of the people he had betrayed.

Eight years after the death of Giacomo Matteotti another momentous assassination took place, this time in Tokyo. The victim was conservative Prime Minister Ki Tsuyoshi Inukai, and the assassins were nine extreme right-wing army and navy officers representing the super-hawkish Japanese military clique. With a single stroke they paved the way for a military takeover of the Japanese government, the most immediate results of which were expansionist aggression in Asia and the Southwest Pacific, and the beginning of a stiff anti-British, anti-American foreign policy. The next step followed logically: the military alliance with Fascist Italy and Nazi Germany. All this led directly to the bombing of Pearl Harbor on December 7, 1941.

We can only speculate on the path America might have taken had the disgruntled bricklayer, Giuseppe Zangara, succeeded in killing President-elect Franklin D. Roosevelt on February 15, 1933 in Miami, Florida. National shock over the attempt was heightened by the fatal wounding of Chicago's mayor, Anton J. Cermak, who received the bullet intended for F.D.R. and died on March 6. Zangara was electrocuted on March 20.

As for the rash of significant assassinations that have occurred around the world over the past twenty years, it is too soon to make positive assessments. Had moderate King Abdullah of Jordan survived the assassin's bullets in 1951, Middle-Eastern politics might well have taken a substantially different course. Had the Puerto Rican Nationalists Oscar Collazo and Griselio Torresola accomplished their avowed desire to assassinate President Harry S Truman in 1950, it is not unreasonable to conjecture that a frightening overreaction might have occurred, led by a fanatical McCarthyite minority.

Certainly the assassinations of such men as Malcolm X, Medgar Evers, and Martin Luther King, Jr., had a devastating impact on the direction of the civil rights movement in the United States. It was in the wake of the murders of John and Robert Kennedy, however, that the American people lost the last vestiges of any national innocence they might have had. For generations they had been force-fed the simplistic myth that the world was divided into "the good guys and the bad guys" and, of course, that "the bad guys" were always the other side. So, in the shattering of the myth, Americans had to face the truth at last: perhaps the cherished innocence had never existed at all.

4

SOCIETY
as the ASSASSIN

The concept of Society as the assassin is, to say the least, a disturbing one. Nevertheless it has many valid facets that must be examined, but first it seems wise to define our terms.

Those embroiled in the age-old controversy over capital punishment would probably consider it alone the subject of this chapter. But capital punishment is dealt with here only as a deliberate instrument to eliminate political or ideological enemies. For example, during the Spanish Inquisition innocent persons were frequently denounced as heretics by unscrupulous individuals, who knew that the denunciations alone carried sufficient weight to cause the victim's execution. During the French Revolution, especially during the Terror, the same thing was done. The chief difference was that in eighteenth-century France the doomed persons were victims of political rather than religious persecution. The fact remains, however, that they were murdered in an atmosphere of sanctimonious righteousness by the society in which they lived.

In modern times the judicial process has been used as

an instrument of murder by totalitarian regimes—both leftist and rightist. When rigidly controlled courts have been used for judicial assassinations, the underlying rationale has always been identical: to give the proceedings an aura of legality for propaganda purposes.

Unfortunately, democratic societies are not altogether innocent. Although it is not common, they, too, occasionally practice the ancient art of assassination in the grim and shadowy world of espionage. Of course, such tactics are employed only as extreme measures when there appears to be no other solution available. Where a functioning democracy has legal jurisdiction, however, there is no need to practice assassination, because the law applies equally to everyone, and legal process is quite able to cope with situations which might require more drastic measures elsewhere. There are many people today, especially in democratic societies, who shy away from all thought of killing and violence. Their attitude is admirable. Perhaps one day they will succeed in their ultimate goal: the abolition of war. But until that time comes, *Homo sapiens* will continue to prove that he is, indeed, the deadliest species of them all.

Why must this be? cry the gentle ones among us. Why should a society, under the guidance of its leaders, deliberately stamp out human life with no more regard for it than for ants, cockroaches, or other pests? The answer is not a simple one. However, in any society where change is not desired by those in power, or where those in power are determined to bring about change by *any* means, bloodshed, terror, and violence are bound to result. Under such conditions assassination is as much a part of political routine as, say, the delivery of mail. Its function, depending upon who utilizes it, is the seizure of power, the

elimination of all competitors or even potential oppo-
nents, and the amalgamation and perpetuation of power
through terrorism.

It should be pointed out here—especially to those who
deliberately disregard the past in order that they may tilt
with more contemporary demons—that no single race,
nationality, religion, or age group has a monopoly on
virtues or vices. The massacres of Armenians by Turks
from 1889 through 1916 were unvarnished genocide, and
cause shudders in the ranks of survivors and their descendants to this day. The late Dominican dictator, Rafael
Trujillo, maintained prisons, torture chambers, and a staff
of assassins on the scale of a Renaissance despot, and
the same can be said for Haiti's present late dictator, François
Duvalier. In pre-Castro Cuba, the dreaded SIM (secret
police) carried out the regime's clandestine murders.
(Once, shortly before the Castro revolution, I was personally forced out of a car at gunpoint on a lonely
road outside Havana, and made to stand with hands up
in the hot sun peering up the gaping muzzle of a sub-
machine gun on the unfounded suspicion that I was smuggling guns. There is no doubt in my mind that had I
made the slightest move toward the man who had me
covered, I would have died in a burst of gunfire.)

Elsewhere in Latin America, to quote Karl Schmitt, of
the University of Texas, "Mexican governments in the
1920's and 1930's certainly strengthened their hold by
ruthlessly exterminating revolutionary and would-be
revolutionary leaders." And in the Middle East it is a
fact of life, even today, that the tradition established
centuries ago by Hassan ibn-al-Sabbah still persists. "For
example," states one of the staff reports to the National
Commission on the Causes and Prevention of Violence,

"King Saud of Saudi Arabia was accused of spending several million dollars in an abortive attempt to kill Nasser."

At no time in history, however, have organized terror and assassination been conducted on such massive proportions as in the Soviet Union under Stalin, and in Nazi Germany during the twelve years of Hitler's Third Reich. Although the Bolshevik Revolution resulted in a left-wing revolutionary regime in Russia, and National Socialism imposed an extreme right-wing government on Germany, the two were strikingly similar insofar as political murder was concerned. Furthermore, despite the fact that each pursued radically different objectives, they were frequently uneasy bedfellows when it was mutually beneficial.

One of the great ironies of all time is that Germany, before the end of World War I, contributed heavily to the success of Bolshevism, its leaders never dreaming at the time that one fateful decision might one day backfire. Nikolai Lenin, the most important Bolshevik leader, was until April 1917 chafing impatiently in Swiss exile. Indeed, the revolution had successfully brought to an end three centuries of oppressive Romanoff rule, but the Bolsheviks were not in control and Russia was floundering for lack of strong leadership. Furthermore, revolution or no, the war was still very much in the shooting stage, and German troops were taking advantage of Russian internal chaos.

Nevertheless, from the official German point of view, the situation was far from rosy, especially in light of rapidly deteriorating relations with the United States. The Kaiser would need all the troops he could muster for service on the Western Front, and his generals knew it. Consequently, when exiled Bolshevik leaders asked German officials to help them get back home, help was enthusiastically given. Lenin turned loose in Russia, it was said, would be more valuable to Germany than two divisions on the Eastern Front. In a sense this was true, for on April 6, 1917, exactly three days after Lenin arrived in Petrograd, the U.S. Congress declared war on Germany, at President Woodrow Wilson's request. Little did anyone dream that, in effect, the decision to send Lenin home began the forging of the sword that would one day slice Germany in two. Not only did Lenin seize absolute control of the revolution and consolidate Bolshevik power, but he was also instrumental in founding the Soviet Union as it is constituted today.

As the Bolsheviks took the reins of power and entrenched themselves, they demonstrated what Machiavelli had stated centuries before, that a state born in violence and bloodshed would evolve the same way. Instead of shrinking from the use of terror, they adapted to it quite naturally. To be sure, they abolished the hated *Okhrana,* or czarist secret police that had terrorized the Russian people since its inception, but this made little difference.

Terrorism, violence, and ruthless suppression of all opposing forces were realities much too familiar in Russia. They were so ingrained in the Russian soul that they could not be expunged overnight. Many Russians may have dreamed about freedom, but they lacked the experience to practice it. Knowledge of musical theory is one thing; playing a musical instrument is another. Therefore, though the revolution itself was a *fait accompli,* a return to autocracy was the only course that could efficiently weld Russia into a nation and hold it together.

The tyranny of the czars was thus replaced by the tyranny of the proletariat.

When the files of the *Okhrana* were taken over, many of its personnel were only too glad to switch their loyalty to new masters in order to keep their skins intact. A new secret police merely took the place of the old. It was called the "All-Russian Extraordinary Commission for the Struggle against Counter-revolution," and was known by the contraction Cheka. The first paragraph of its constitution authorized it to "prevent and liquidate all attempts at counter-revolution or sabotage throughout the territory of the Russian Empire from whatever quarter they may originate."

Furthermore, on February 22, 1918, the Bolshevik leadership stated officially that it saw

> no other measures to fight counter-revolutionaries, spies, speculators, ruffians, hooligans, saboteurs, and other parasites than merciless annihilation on the spot of the offense and therefore declares that all . . . will be mercilessly shot by the commission's detachments on the spot of the offense.[1]

As "the commission's detachments" (as the murder squads were so euphemistically called) went about exchanging new terror for old, one of Lenin's more sanguine theories was put into practice; namely that "Socialist revolution is impossible without the extermination of a certain section of the bourgeoisie."

Soon, however, the inevitable happened. As Lenin's health began to fail, the most ambitious of his would-be political heirs gathered and steeled themselves for the power struggle that was bound to ensue. In the spring of 1922 two significant events took place. The Cheka was formally dissolved and replaced by the GPU, or State

Political Directorate, and Joseph Stalin was named Secretary General of the Communist Party. When Lenin, the founding father, died in 1924, Stalin seized power and became absolute master of the Soviet Union.

In order to consolidate and maintain power, Stalin had to make drastic and bloody moves. Former heroes of the revolution were either murdered or forced into exile. What happened is neatly summed up by Feliks Gross in his report to the Eisenhower Commission in 1969:

> Political assassination in the Soviet Union was institutionalized in the form of mass terror, and legitimized by ideology. It is beyond the scope of this essay to discuss the political assassinations performed on Stalin's order in various countries. Stalin's massive scale calls for volumes, not chapters. The assassination of Sergei Kirov, in 1934, friend of Stalin and member of the Politburo, was the beginning of the great purges in which thousands of innocent people were executed. The assassination of Kirov still remains a mysterious affair. The purge trials and executions were, in fact, judicial assassinations.
>
> Until this time, however, the mass terror instituted soon after Soviet seizure of power continued with varying intensity. During the Civil War, White troops, fighting the young Soviet Republic, practiced their own "White Terror," and massacred whomever they captured and suspected.
>
> The internecine carnage during the period of the Revolution calls for a special study of the human potentialities for violence and brutality. Individual assassinations in such a climate become, because of their sheer numbers, quantitative statistics. In human destiny, an individual act is the measure of the man, and a window to an understanding of his mind. Quantity or vast numbers alone cannot reveal this.[2]

Nevertheless, numbers do give an indication of how far a state can go in implementing an official policy of assassination and terror against those it considers to be its enemies. Between the spring of 1937 and the fall of

1938 the highest estimate of total military liquidations was a staggering sixty-one percent of the top ranks. This figure included only those men holding ranks from Division Commander up to Marshal of the Soviet Union. Thirty thousand officers are reported to have lost their lives in this period. Outside the army, others said to have been either executed, murdered, or to have committed suicide under duress included all the Deputy Commissars of Defense, the chiefs of the naval and air forces, the head of the Military Political Administration and his deputy chief, along with most of their lower ranking counterparts in all Soviet military districts, the Director of the Frunze Military Academy, the head of the Society of Associates for Aviation and Chemical Defense, and all naval fleet commanders except one. In view of such a decimation of its officer corps, the Red Army's ability to withstand Hitler's onslaughts only a few years later is a tribute, not only to the fierce determination of the common soldiers, but to the capabilities of relatively inexperienced leadership in the upper echelons.

By the time World War II broke out, the Soviet apparatus for extermination had undergone a number of changes. The GPU had become the OGPU in another reorganization. This in turn was dissolved in 1934 and its functions taken over by a People's Commissariat of Internal Affairs, better known as the NKVD. Upheavals continued to occur. After Stalin died in 1953 the NKVD became part of the Ministry of Internal Affairs (the MVD). At that time the Committee of State Security (the KGB) was set up to coordinate the activities of all security services.

Buried deep within the complicated maze comprising the Soviet security web is the so-called Special Division. It traces its ancestry to a section of the old Cheka, whose agents were called the *Istrebiteli,* or exterminators. A bureaucracy in itself, with headquarters in Moscow's notorious Lubyanka Prison, the Special Division has a number of sections. Only one of them—the ninth—is of particular interest here. It has been known by many names, including "The Section for Terror and Diversion." But between the years 1941 and 1947 it was called SMERSH, which is a contraction of the Russian phrase *Smert Shpionam,* meaning "death to spies." Although its name was later changed to the less ominous sounding VKR (*Vodennaya Kontr Rozvedka*), meaning "Organization for Counter-Infiltration," the more colorful SMERSH has stuck unofficially. It should be acknowledged, however, that had it not been for the late Ian Fleming's James Bond novels, the name would never have gained such widespread public notoriety.

Though the name itself has been sinister enough, the activities of its agents over the years have been infinitely more so. A full count of SMERSH victims will probably never be made for a number of reasons, not the least significant of which is the high sophistication of its weapons and special equipment. Although there is no way of proving it, knowledgeable individuals believe that the man who assassinated Leon Trotsky in 1940 was an agent of SMERSH. The weapon he used was anything but subtle—a pickaxe of the kind used by alpine mountain climbers. But it was just as effective as silenced cigarette-case pistols and lethal, odorless, fast-acting gases. The postscript to Trotsky's assassination was written when his enigmatic killer was released from prison in Mexico in 1963. There was still no clue as to his actual identity. Whether he was really Ramón Mercador, Frank Jacson, or Jacques Mornard (his various aliases) may never be

SOCIETY AS THE ASSASSIN   69

known for certain. What is known, however, is that officials
of the Czechoslovakian Embassy in Mexico put him on a
plane for Cuba, where he was royally entertained by the
Castro government. Later, he went to Prague and then
to Moscow. He has not been seen by anyone in the West
since.

Extensive as the Soviet use of terror and assassination
was in the past, events of recent years have indicated a
Russian tendency to become more conservative. The
people of the U.S.S.R. are neither hungry nor particularly
afraid. A rigidly controlled press limits their information,
and they have learned through hard experience that
obedience is preferable to the sort of punishment meted
out to those who get out of line (e.g. the two writers Yuli
Daniel and Andrei Sinkyavsky, who were imprisoned for
the "crime" of publishing pseudonymously in the West).
Thus, the apparatus of terror remains, and its technology
undergoes continuous refinement. Above all, it is ready
for use whenever it may be called upon.

Unlike the Bolsheviks, the Nazis did not come to power
by means of an uprising that overthrew the existing
government. They were certainly revolutionary in nature,
but they were voted into power by the enthusiastic elec-
torate that comprised Germany's silent majority. Emerging
from obscurity in Vienna, Hitler had gone to Germany
in the gloomy days that followed defeat in World War I.
Shortly after joining the infant National Socialist German
Workers Party, he became its master as the first step in
his design to conquer the world. *Today We Rule Germany, Tomorrow the World,* was a familiar Nazi slogan
of the time. Leading the Nazi party in its whirlwind rise
of hate-mongering and terrorism, he combined dema-
goguery with shrewd psychology, appealing to the dis-

contented, the embittered, and the disenfranchised masses. He spelled out his master plan for world conquest and mass murder well in advance, in *Mein Kampf,* but the extravagant promises he made in his book were so fantastic that no one believed him. When he and his henchmen finally controlled Europe they surpassed the Russians in both the theory and practice of terror, and by the time of their collapse in 1945 their victims could be counted in millions.

In the beginning, the principal targets for Nazi assassins were persons (mostly German) who, for any reason, seemed to stand in Hitler's way. Unlike other political parties, the Nazis had organized their own private army, which in the early years of struggle was one of their chief instruments for bludgeoning their way to power. The brown-shirted S.A. (*Sturmabteilung*), or storm troops, were nothing more than a semi-disciplined gang of uniformed thugs and hoodlums whose top leadership had in its ranks a number of men with criminal records. The specialties of the S.A. included street brawling, rioting, massive intimidation of political adversaries, and terrorism in general. They were equally adept at beating up elderly Jews and murdering healthy Christians.

The last democratic elections to be held in Germany until after World War II, were on March 5, 1933. The Nazi Party led the field with 17,277,180 votes. After blaming the Communists for the Reichstag Fire (Hermann Goering later privately boasted of having struck the match himself), Hitler made himself effective dictator of Germany by pushing through a so-called Enabling Act, which placed all power in the hands of the cabinet, which he as Chancellor controlled. Next, in rapid succession, opposition political parties were abolished, trade unions dissolved, the traditional German states were deprived of their powers, anti-Jewish laws were passed, and censorship was tightened.

In all of these moves the S.A. played a vital role. By 1934 its ranks had grown to unwieldy proportions, numbering between two and a half and three million men. Their paramilitary structure, their numbers, and their excessive behavior now began to stir up alarm abroad. Anthony Eden, then Lord Privy Seal of Great Britain, concerned that the S.A., because of its size, might be in violation of the Versailles Treaty, visited Berlin in February 1934 and extracted a promise from Hitler to reduce its ranks from the current strength to approximately 750,000. Hitler was actually anxious to comply for two very different reasons: First, he secretly admired the British and was anxious to curry favor with them at this time; second, he was well aware of the growing fears in the ranks of the traditional Prussian military caste. The generals were jealous of their time-honored position in German society, and they regarded the S.A. with contempt. It was not unreasonable to assume that if the S.A. became too strong in the eyes of the generals they might stage a *coup* and seize the government. No one was more aware of this than Hitler himself.

To compound the growing problem, the S.A.'s arrogant hooliganism was increasing. They were so drunk with their own power that few dared to get in their way. Furthermore, their leader, Ernst Roehm, had been making what could only be described as dangerous noises. He was calling for a "second revolution." This alarmed the military clique, the junker class, and the wealthy industrialists, all of whom had contributed one way or another to the rise of Nazism. A second revolution could conceivably put them all out of business. From Hitler's point of view this spelled trouble. If Roehm and his S.A. staged a successful *coup,* his own future was uncertain, and if the industrialists, the junkers, and the generals ganged up on him, the Nazi Party and the Third Reich would be finished.

Hitler's decision could not have been a difficult one. The S.A. had served its purpose. As William L. Shirer said, in *The Rise and Fall of the Third Reich,* "The S.A. was but a mob—good enough for street fighting but of little worth as a modern army." Contrary to the terms of the Versailles Treaty, Germany was building a clandestine new war machine as rapidly as possible, ironically, despite official anti-communist utterances, with the aid of the Soviet Union. Much of the military hardware was being manufactured secretly in Russia, and considerable illegal training of future Nazi armed forces was also taking place there.

Roehm was no fool, and he could see which way the winds were blowing. He had one ace, however. As one of Hitler's oldest personal friends, and a key figure in the rise of Nazism, he was still a man to be reckoned with. In a bold bid for even greater power, he proposed at a cabinet meeting that the S.A. become the nucleus for a new German army, and that the entire armed force be reorganized, and placed under the jurisdiction of a single ministry with himself at its head. This was more than his enemies could take. Thus, not only did he effectively set up his own downfall, but he put into motion a series of events that would lead to the first large-scale Nazi massacre to shake the world—the Blood Purge of June 30, 1934.

It is not necessary here to go into the tangled intrigues

immediately prior to the purge. Suffice it to say that Hitler made a deal with the generals at a meeting aboard the naval cruiser *Deutschland* on May 16, 1934. He promised to defang the S.A., if not to completely crush it, if the military establishment would agree in return to back him all the way in the future. The scales were tipped in favor of Roehm's death during a general massacre when Hermann Goering and Heinrich Himmler joined forces to ensure the elimination of their hated rival. But the most significant long-range result of the collaboration between this pair was twofold: the separation of the black-clad S.S. (*Schutzstaffel*, or elite guards) from the S.A., of which they had originally been merely a part; and the creation of the Gestapo. Actually, the Gestapo (*Geheime Staats-Polizei*, or Secret State Police) came into being before the Blood Purge, and indeed was very active in carrying it out. But only after the purge did its sweeping powers make it, in partnership with the S.S., Hitler's most effective instrument of terror and mass murder.

As June 30 approached, Goering and Himmler worked feverishly to convince Hitler that Roehm was plotting against him, for without the approval of *Der Fuehrer,* their own machinations would fail. Nevertheless, they set the stage, counting on success. Lists of proposed victims were carefully drawn up, including many who had nothing to do with Roehm or the S.A., but who had been marked for liquidation by the two conspirators for purely personal reasons.

Finally, less than a week before the fatal day, Hitler was won over, and his last-minute entries were added to the death lists. The army did its part on June 25. On that day General von Fritsch, the commander-in-chief, cancelled all leaves and ordered all troops confined to barracks. This left a clear field for Gestapo and S.S. murder squads who were secretly mobilized on June 28.

As those who were to die went about their normal business on Friday night, June 29, none of them had the slightest inkling that he would not survive the weekend. Many, in fact, were planning vacations and outings, largely because Roehm had issued an order giving the entire S.A. all of July off. This was certainly not indicative of an organization on the verge of staging a *coup d'état*. Yet, by Monday morning the purge was over, and Hitler had demonstrated with a single stroke that the world had better take him seriously. He had said: "I shall spread terror by employing the element of surprise in all my measures." And, "The important thing is the sudden shock of an overwhelming fear of death." Even more specific was his declaration that "Natural instincts bid all living things not merely to conquer their enemies, but to destroy them. . . . We must be ruthless."[3]

More than one thousand persons perished (according to testimony at the belated trial of available defendants in Munich, in May 1957). But for those who survived the worst was yet to come.

On Tuesday, July 3, General Werner von Blomberg, Minister of Defense, congratulated Hitler, and the cabinet passed a resolution approving the bloody massacre as having been necessary for "the defense of the state." The lengths to which Hitler was prepared to go in "defending the state" obviously exceeded Blomberg's limited imagination and, indeed, that of the combined brains of the entire general staff. For they maintained until the very end that they had believed themselves capable of dealing with the grubby Austrian ex-corporal. But they underestimated him and overestimated themselves, especially

when each swore a personal oath of allegiance to Adolf
Hitler as Chancellor and *Fuehrer* after the death of the
aged President von Hindenburg on August 2.

For Heinrich Himmler especially, this marked the turning point in his remarkable career as Hitler's chief ex-
terminator of human beings. The words of the poet,
Heinrich Heine, written over a hundred years earlier, now
gleamed more intensely than the flames that had con-
sumed them during the infamous book burning of 1933:
"Wherever they burn books, sooner or later they burn
human beings also."

Among those who may not be thoroughly familiar with
the Third Reich's short, bloody history, the question may
arise: In light of the wholesale slaughters eventually per-
petrated by the Nazis, why single out a relatively minor
massacre like the June 30th purge? The answer is simple.
This initial mass assassination effectively terrorized and
silenced many who might otherwise have given Hitler
and the Nazis stiff opposition. Furthermore, it set a
precedent for the future *modus operandi* of the S.S. and
the Gestapo.

So much has been written about these two infamous
organizations and their principal *dramatis personae* that
only a brief outline is necessary here. At the top of the
pyramid was Himmler himself, bearing the title *Reichs-
fuehrer.* The only two of his high-ranking lieutenants
who need be mentioned here are Reinhard Heydrich and
Heinrich Mueller. The latter ran the Gestapo until the
very end when he disappeared without a trace, indicating
that he may very well have survived. He was a colorless,
but efficient administrator, who kept strictly out of politics,
thus ensuring a high degree of invulnerability to internecine
intrigue.

Heydrich was a story in himself. Bearing the nickname

"Hangman," he was an evil genius who created much of the structural organization of the Nazi police and intelligence network. Among other things, he headed what amounted to an elite corps within the S.S.—the S.D., or *Sicherheitsdienst.* Technically the name meant "Security Service," but actually it functioned essentially as the intelligence arm of the Gestapo, being so inextricably related to it that in retrospect it is difficult to separate the two. Heydrich had the talents of a brilliant administrator and the instincts of a sadistic murderer, and is credited with being the brains behind the so-called "Final Solution" or extermination of the Jews, which was so efficiently managed by his subordinate Adolf Eichmann. The supreme irony about Heydrich is that he was tall, fair, and handsome, personifying the Nazi concept of the perfect "pure Aryan." Yet, though he kept it a closely guarded secret, he was one-quarter Jewish. Himmler, of course, upon learning this fact, reported it to Hitler, who in turn demanded an immediate interview with Heydrich.

After a long private conversation the Fuehrer dismissed Heydrich and confided afterward to Himmler that the future Gauleiter of Bohemia and Moravia was a "highly gifted" but "highly dangerous" man whose talents had to be devoted exclusively to the Nazi cause. Such men, Hitler declared, could be allowed to exist only if held firmly under the thumb, and Heydrich's Jewish blood was the ideal sword of Damocles to hold over his head. Of the outcome, Charles Wighton wrote in his book, *Heydrich: Hitler's Most Evil Henchman:*

> Himmler then said that Heydrich had been "eternally thankful" to both Hitler and himself for keeping him in the Party after this discovery. In consequence, he would obey any order blindly and Hitler used him ruthlessly. The Fuehrer entrusted Heydrich with

all the assignments which no one else would touch, with complete
confidence that Heydrich would carry them out to perfection.[4]

Heydrich died as he lived, in violence, at the hands of
Czechoslovakian partisans who had been trained and
armed by the British, then dropped by parachute with
all the necessary equipment. This was in June 1942.
Himmler was actually relieved to see him out of the way,
for he had been a very ambitious young man. Nevertheless, in retaliation for his assassination the Gestapo per-
petrated some of their most deplorable atrocities.

> 1,331 Czechs (including 201 women) were executed.
> 3,000 Jews were deported from the so-called "privileged ghetto"
> of Theresienstadt to an extermination camp.
> 500 Jews were arrested in Berlin. 152 of whom were summarily
> executed.
> The men and boys more than sixteen years old from the Czech
> village of Lidice were rounded up and shot: total, 172 (19 others
> were later deported). Of the women, 7 were shot, 7 were gassed
> at Ravensbrueck, 42 died of ill treatment, and 3 are unaccounted for.
> Four pregnant women were permitted to give birth at Prague, but
> immediately afterward their infants were murdered and the women
> were sent to concentration camps. All the children who survived
> were rounded up and given what the S.S. men lightly called "the
> racial once-over." If they were sufficiently nonSlavic in appearance,
> they were sent to be raised as Germans with selected Nazi families.
> The rest were "disposed of."
> The town of Lidice was torn down so that not one stone would
> be left standing on another, and in order that its memory might
> be erased from the mind of mankind.

Lidice today is one of Czechoslovakia's most solemn
memorials to her war dead.
Between them, the S.S. and the Gestapo had the most
awesome powers ever granted to any military or police
organizations in history. Certainly, had it not been for

Himmler's fanatical devotion to Hitler and the Nazi cause, they could have seized the government at any time they chose to stage a *coup* of their own. Of course, they, too, engaged in vicious infighting among themselves in constant power struggles. A former Gestapo man, Hans Bernd Gisevius, who survived, wrote a book about it, in which he said:

> It was so usual for members of the Gestapo to arrest one another that we scarcely took notice of such incidents, unless we happened to come across a more detailed example of such an arrest—by way of the hospital or the morgue.[5]

The statute that legalized their activities specifically stated that they were above the law. Whatever decisions they made in regard to individuals were final. There was no appeal from those decisions, and the judiciary was not authorized to examine them. Finally, even though a person might have been tried and acquitted by a court, he could be arrested immediately afterward by the Gestapo and imprisoned or executed without benefit of trial.

"The spirit of the matter," wrote Edward Crankshaw in *The Gestapo,* "is best conveyed in the words of Hitler's notorious proclamation of 22nd October 1938: '. . . every means adopted for carrying out the will of the Leader is considered legal, even though it may conflict with existing statutes and precedents.' "[6]

In other words, Adolf Hitler's will, whatever the state of his sanity, was the only law.

Within Germany and beyond its borders they carried out a deliberate policy best described by a word favored by Hitler, *Schrecklichkeit*—frightfulness. They engineered assassinations of political figures abroad, notably that of Austrian Prime Minister Engelbert Dollfuss, as a prelude to the abortive attempt to seize the Austrian government from within. And though they might not have conducted the operation themselves, the Gestapo most certainly lent assistance to the Croatian terrorists who assassinated King Alexander I of Yugoslavia and French Foreign Minister Jean Louis Barthou in Marseille, in 1934, thereby paving the way for the assumption of office by pro-Nazis in both countries.

But perhaps the best summation of their activities as official murderers working on behalf of Hitler's Reich comes from the records of the Nuremberg Trials, where it was given by an American prosecutor, Colonel Story.

> The Gestapo and the S.D. played an important part in almost every criminal act of the conspiracy [i.e. the Nazi conspiracy]. The category of these crimes, apart from the thousands of specific instances of torture and cruelty in policing Germany for the benefit of the conspirators, reads like a page from the devil's notebook.
>
> They fabricated the border incidents which Hitler used as an excuse for attacking Poland.
>
> They murdered hundreds of thousands of defenseless men, women, and children by the infamous Einsatz [Special Action] groups.
>
> They removed Jews, political leaders, and scientists from prisoner-of-war camps and murdered them.
>
> They took recaptured prisoners-of-war to concentration camps and murdered them.
>
> They established and classified the concentration camps and sent thousands of people into them for extermination and slave labor.
>
> They cleared Europe of Jews and were responsible for sending hundreds of thousands to their deaths in annihilation camps.
>
> They rounded up hundreds of thousands of citizens of occupied countries and shipped them to Germany for forced labor and sent slave laborers to labor reformatory camps.
>
> They executed captured commandos and paratroopers, and protected civilians who lynched Allied fliers.
>
> They took civilians of occupied countries to Germany for secret trial and punishment.

They arrested, tried, and punished citizens of occupied countries under special criminal procedures which did not accord fair trials, and by summary methods.

They murdered or sent to concentration camps the relatives of persons who had allegedly committed crimes.

They ordered the murder of prisoners in Sipo [Security police] and S.D. prisons to prevent their release by Allied armies.

They participated in the seizure and spoliation of public and private property.

They were the primary agents for the persecution of the Jews and the churches.[7]

What so many have continually failed to understand is how the men who carried out these atrocities and mass murders could calmly disclaim responsibility by saying that they were merely following orders. A clue might be found in an extract from a speech made by Hermann Goering in the early days, when he was still chief of the Prussian Gestapo.

Every bullet which leaves the barrel of a police pistol now is my bullet. If one calls this murder, then I have murdered: I ordered all this. I back it up. I assume the responsibility, and I am not afraid to do so.[8]

A number of men were hanged at Nuremberg for their responsibilities in those crimes against humanity whether they admitted them or not, for the evidence was overwhelmingly against them. Yet, had they been the victors, might they not have been the hangmen instead of the prisoners?

5

PORTRAIT of the ASSASSIN as a MADMAN

If it were possible to analyze in detail every political assassination over the past two hundred years, and feed into a computer all the pertinent facts about each assassin, we would find that a startling number of them were completely insane. Yet, owing largely to the intensity of public emotion in the wake of a prominent individual's assassination, it was not until 1843 that society was sufficiently mature to find a man not guilty of murder by reason of insanity.

The London jury that announced this startling verdict, in addition to setting a legal precedent, created a sensation of scandalous proportions. Not only did its decision unleash a torrent of unfavorable criticism from both public and press, but it provoked heated debates in Parliament, particularly in the House of Lords. Finally it gave rise to a set of rules that lawyers on both sides of the Atlantic have been arguing about ever since—the McNaughton Rules. The most authoritative wording of the rules, written at the time, states essentially that:

> The jurors ought to be told in all cases that every man is to be presumed to be sane, and to possess a sufficient degree of reason to be responsible for his crimes, until the contrary be proved to their satisfaction; and that, to establish a defense on the ground of insanity, it must be proved that at the time of the committing of the act, the party accused was laboring under such a defect of reason, from disease of the mind, as not to know the nature and quality of the act he was doing; or, if he did know it, that he did not know he was doing what was wrong.[1]

But what of the man who gave the rules their name? In legal and medical histories he appears only as a shadowy, faceless figure. Daniel McNaughton, the principal player in one of the most significant courtroom dramas in legal history, stands enshrouded in an obscurity he does not deserve. For, when we examine him closely, we gain better knowledge of the tortured mind of the assassin who kills, not for any rational motive, but because he is mentally ill.

McNaughton was a young Scot who intended to kill Sir Robert Peel, the British Prime Minister, but who made an error and killed Peel's secretary instead. Fortunately all the facts are recorded. The dusty transcripts of the proceedings at Old Bailey are still in the London Public Records Office. The newspapers of the day, though crumbling around the edges and musty smelling, tell us as exciting a story today as they did when the early editions were first hawked on the streets. Most apparent in these browned old journals are the feelings and emotions of the time. They are feelings and emotions which, if the crime had occurred in another milieu—say in America of the old West or the South—might have resulted in a lynching—without benefit of law. But this was England, and the time was 1843, the sixth year of young Queen Victoria's reign.

London on Friday, January 20, 1843 was cloudy and damp. A light north wind swept gray fog through the city, and as the sweepers readied the Princess Theatre on Oxford Street for the evening's performance of *Lucia di Lammermoor,* the curtain was rising on a real-life mad scene in Whitehall.

At exactly 3:30 P.M. two well-dressed gentlemen, Mr. Edward Drummond, secretary to the Prime Minister, and his friend the Earl of Haddington, left Downing Street and headed in the general direction of Charing Cross. At the Admiralty the Earl left Drummond, who proceeded alone to his brother's bank, which was situated in the immediate vicinity. Not more than fifteen minutes elapsed between the time Drummond entered and left the bank and then retraced his steps along the familiar route to Downing Street. Walking casually along the sidewalk, Drummond was totally unaware that he was being followed. Trailing him at a distance of about three yards was a thin, unobtrusive young man who stood about 5'10", and who wore ordinary-looking dun-colored trousers and a black coat. His only distinguishing feature was an extremely ruddy complexion. Soon the man quickened his pace and began to close the gap between himself and Drummond. When they were passing the Salopian Coffee House, halfway between the Admiralty and the Horse Guards, the man in the black coat, now at Drummond's heels, reached suddenly inside of his coat, whipped out a pistol, jammed the muzzle in his victim's back, and fired.

With a look of pained astonishment on his face, Drummond clutched his side and lurched forward. His assailant stepped calmly back, pocketed the discharged pistol, and reached under his coat for another. Just as he was aiming to fire a second shot, Constable James Silver rushed for-

ward and grappled with him. To Silver's amazement, the
would-be assassin struggled fiercely, not trying to escape,
but obviously attempting to fire another shot at Drummond. The scuffle was brief, for a passerby, Benjamin
Weston, hastened to the constable's aid. Weston seized
the determined gunman by the collar and held fast as
Silver deflected the hand clutching the pistol. The weapon
went off in midair, causing the ball to go wild. Seconds
later the constable succeeded in subduing the attacker and
making him a prisoner.

Meanwhile a small crowd had gathered. Drummond did
not appear to be badly hurt. His coat, blackened and
singed by the point-blank pistol shot, seemed to have
suffered most of the damage. The wound was not bleeding profusely and, with the aid of a stranger, he was able
to walk to his brother's bank. A physician was summoned
immediately. Diagnosing the injury as slight, he ordered
a cab and sent Drummond home to his house on Grosvenor
Street.

At home Drummond's physician, Dr. G. J. Guthrie, along
with two colleagues, Doctors Richard Jackson and Bransby
Cooper, made a more thorough examination. The ball had
entered the back near the spine and had narrowly missed
the stomach, near which it lodged. The doctors were relieved that no vital organ appeared to have been damaged, and they agreed that the best course of action was
to probe for the bullet and remove it. After this was accomplished, Drummond seemed to rest more easily and
Dr. Guthrie assured the press that his patient's wound
was not serious, and he would most assuredly live.

While the doctors were attending to Drummond, Constable Silver's prisoner was the center of attraction at the
Gardiner's Lane police station. Although he was ques-

tioned intensively, he steadfastly refused to reveal anything more than his name, Daniel McNaughton. The
police assumed from his accent that he was a Scot, although someone suggested the possibility of his being a
Northern Irishman. Since it was obvious that he intended
to say nothing more at the time, a hearing was set for ten
o'clock the next morning at Bow Street Court, Magistrate
Hall presiding.

Before he was led to a cell, McNaughton's possessions
were taken from him and inventoried. It was duly noted
that the prisoner had on his person two five-pound notes,
four pounds in gold, a key, a knife, ten percussion caps,
and a receipt from the Glasgow and Ship Bank showing
a recent deposit of £750. It was the last item that took
McNaughton out of the realm of ordinary prisoners, for
the purchasing power of such a bank balance made him a
relatively affluent young man.

The press reaction to the affair was one of utter shock.
Although an obscure man as far as the public was concerned, Edward Drummond was a highly placed official
with a spotless reputation. Not only did he have access
to closely guarded state secrets, but he enjoyed the complete confidence of all the cabinet ministers, and it was
whispered about that he exerted a far greater influence
in Whitehall than might be expected of a man in his
position. Drummond came from an old family that had a
number of peers in its background, as well as a long-
standing history of loyalty to the crown. News of the shooting reached his brother, Colonel Berkeley Drummond of
the Scots Fusilier Life Guards, as he was dining with the
Queen, to whom he was Groom-in-waiting.

Everyone from Her Majesty to the man in the street
was horrified. Why had this obviously well-to-do man at-

tempted such a senseless crime? What possible motive could he have had for shooting Sir Robert Peel's private secretary? If anyone suspected that the bullet had been intended for the Prime Minister, he did not speak. And the only person who could answer the question, McNaughton himself, did not choose, as yet, to reveal anything.

The *Times* of London seemed anxious to convict him at once, before trial. In the morning edition of January 21, 1843, the day after the shooting, the first salvo was fired. It was an obvious attempt to make a case for McNaughton's sanity, almost as though the paper were afraid the question might arise and spoil its campaign. Of his arrest the *Times* said:

> The prisoner was well, though not genteelly dressed . . . his demeanour throughout was cool and collected, nor did there appear to be any evidence of insanity.

As Londoners read the story of the shooting in their morning papers, a tense drama began to unfold in Magistrate Hall's Bow Street courtroom. Two police inspectors led McNaughton before the bench at 10 A.M. for his initial hearing. The *Times* reporter, scribbling away on his pad, noted that the prisoner did not appear to be at all ferocious. When questioned by Magistrate Hall, McNaughton answered respectfully in a soft voice that was heavily accented with a thick, Scottish burr. He gave his age as 27, his occupation as turner (i.e. a lathe worker), and his address as 7 Poplar Row, Newington. After providing these sparse personal details, he made no further statements. The witnesses who had been called, however, had a good deal to say. Constable Silver, who had made the arrest, gave a detailed, accurate account of what had happened, adding only, "As I led the prisoner away I heard him say 'He' or 'she'—I don't remember which—'shall not destroy my peace of mind any longer.' "

Benjamin Weston, the man who had assisted the constable during the arrest, corroborated Silver's story, and another witness, bystander Robert Hodges, testified that McNaughton had followed Drummond for quite a distance before shooting him in the back. Finally, another constable, James Partridge, whose testimony later on was to give strong ammunition to the prosecution, testified that he had seen the prisoner loitering in the vicinity of Whitehall for the past seventeen or eighteen days. However, according to the reports, McNaughton failed to recognize Constable Partridge.

After the testimony of the witnesses, McNaughton was asked if there was any statement he might care to make in his own behalf, but he quietly refused. Magistrate Hall then ordered him removed to a cell and held there for two weeks pending further action by the authorities. Looking neither to the right nor to the left, McNaughton was led from the courtroom under guard, but when they reached his cell he changed his mind. "I want to talk to the judge," he said.

He was immediately returned to the courtroom and brought back before the bench. The spectators and reporters, who had begun to leave, hurried back to their places and strained to hear every word, for the prisoner spoke in the same low voice he had used before but, for the first time since his arrest, he talked at length.

"The Tories in my native city have compelled me to do this," he said. "They follow me and persecute me wherever I go, and have entirely destroyed my peace of mind. They followed me to France, into Scotland, and all over England. In fact, they follow me wherever I go, I

can get no rest from them night or day." There was a
look of genuine anguish on his face as he paused, wiped
his forehead with his sleeve, and continued. "I cannot
sleep at nights in consequence of the course they pursue
towards me. I believe they have driven me into a consumption, I am sure I shall never be the man I formerly
was. I used to have good health and strength, but I have
not now. They have accused me of crimes of which I am
not guilty. They have done everything in their power to
harass and persecute me, in fact they wish to murder me.
It can be proved by evidence . . ." His voice seemed to
trail off.

"Is that all you wish to say?" asked the clerk.

McNaughton hesitated and looked around. "I can only
say that they have completely disordered my mind, and I
am not capable of doing anything compared to what I
was." He paused and lowered his eyes. "I am a very
different man to what I was before they commenced their
system of persecution."

"Do you wish to say anything more?" the clerk asked
again.

At that McNaughton glanced in the direction of the
cells. "Oh, yes," he replied, pointing his finger. "I wish
to know whether I am to be kept in that place for a fort-
night? If so, I'm sure I won't live!"

Although the wretched conditions of nineteenth-century
London jails may have aroused McNaughton's fears for his
continued existence, he ultimately had no cause for alarm.
Instead of being placed in a cell, he was confined to the
jailor's room, where it was later reported that he was
cheerful, well behaved, and possessed of a hearty appetite.
Whether or not McNaughton's affluent financial status
had anything to do with his comfortable confinement is a

matter for speculation. In any case it was noted by those around him that never once during this entire period did he mention the crime, or behave in what might be construed as an irrational manner.

Meanwhile, a warrant was obtained and McNaughton's living quarters were searched. His landlady, Mrs. Elizabeth Dutton, was a respectable widow with whom Daniel McNaughton had lived for three years. When he first came to London from Scotland he had lodged with her and proven, as far as she was concerned, to be a perfect lodger. Not only was he sober and quiet, but he always paid his two shillings sixpence a week promptly. Although he had left London on several occasions, he always returned to Poplar Row and occupied the same quarters, the back room on the second floor. Mrs. Dutton told the police that in her opinion he was a rather poor fellow. First of all, he left the house every morning no later than nine o'clock, presumably to seek work. Secondly, he had no boxes of belongings in his room; and lastly, he had very few articles of clothing.

"He had one pair of boots to his name," she declared. "I recall once he asked me to lend him a pair while his were being mended at the bootmaker's."

It was quite plain that widow Dutton thought well of her young Scottish lodger "even if he was a bit on the gloomy side." His extreme taciturnity she attributed to "something on his mind." When asked if she thought that McNaughton might possibly be insane, Mrs. Dutton strenuously rejected the suggestion. He was far too polite to be a madman, she insisted.

"Tight with a shilling, he might be," she admitted, "but after all, what else might you expect from a Scot?"

To illustrate her point she told as much about his fru-

gality as she could—how he never brought home a newspaper or a book, yet, how he was anxious to borrow them
whenever possible. As she enthusiastically told the police
how much McNaughton enjoyed reading her personal
copy of *Excerpts from the Bible* they interrupted to pursue
a more profitable line of questioning. What, if anything,
they asked, had he ever mentioned about politics? Mrs.
Dutton thought about it for a moment, then brightly recalled that he had told her how his last visit to Scotland
had coincided with that of Queen Victoria. Apparently
he never mentioned the Tories or the Prime Minister,
and the name Edward Drummond had meant nothing
to her at all until she had read it in the newspaper.

Realizing that they had gone as far as possible with
their interrogation, the police began to search the sparsely
furnished room. It took very little time to find exactly
what they had come for: a powder horn, a sizable quantity
of percussion caps, and most important of all, a number
of newly cast lead balls that fit Daniel McNaughton's
pistols perfectly.

While all of this was taking place, Edward Drummond's
condition grew progressively worse. He was visited by
his brother, who brought a message from the royal household expressing wishes for a speedy recovery. Later on,
Sir Robert Peel came to call. Although there is no record
of what was said during that visit, doubtless the Prime
Minister had a fairly good idea that the bullet which had
felled his secretary had been intended for him. Not only
did he have numerous political enemies as head of a conservative government, but there were unquestionably
many denizens of the London underworld who would
be happy to see him dead. Sir Robert's reorganization of
the London police force had been so effective that its

members had already acquired the nicknames of "Bobby" and "Peeler."

By Monday morning the nation was clamoring with indignation over the shooting. A *Times* editorial expressed this reaction with typical early-Victorian grandiloquence, saying:

> Can it be that we are approaching that fearful period in a nation's history when men become indifferent to right and wrong— when patience, charity, and patriotism give way to private revenge and selfish malice,—when all thought and care for the honour of their country are merged in a rabid appetite for an evil notoriety, or in a morbid craving after desperate vengeance? God forbid! We had rather see England reft of all her glory, greatness, and possessions, than tarnished with the crimes of ancient Venice, or dishonoured by the wickedness of modern France.

What horrified *Times* editorial writers was not so much the shooting of one man by another, but the fact that a public figure might be stalked and shot down in the streets of London for political reasons. Since Drummond was not well known to the public, they guessed correctly that he had been shot by mistake. Although they did not speculate on who the intended victim might have been, they did conjecture somewhat grudgingly that McNaughton might be a madman rather than a political partisan "whose passions had gotten the better of him." They alluded to his violent outbursts against his persecutors, the Tories, and expressed a hope that the former possibility was the correct assumption, otherwise . . .

> We cannot abstain from expressing our horror, not only at the present atrocious attempt, whoever may have been its designed victim, but at the dreadful imputation which this and similar attempts have fixed upon the national character.

As self-proclaimed guardian of the national character, the *Times* claimed that it would prefer to discover that the man who shot Drummond was insane. The paper went out of its way, however, to sneer at any suggestion that McNaughton might be able to wear that label, despite its own previous statement that he might be mad. The paper hinted that his statement about being persecuted by the Tories was merely a stratagem designed to convince the authorities of his insanity. Besides, said the *Times,* a strong anti-Tory attitude, like a strong anti-income tax attitude, could hardly be considered insanity.

On Tuesday, January 24, the papers somberly reported that Drummond's condition had taken a turn for the worse and was now critical. The next morning, the *Times* combined its usual pompous verbosity with genuine regret:

> Our columns of this morning confirm the worst fears that were entertained of Mr. Drummond's fate. He is no more.

About McNaughton, it said:

> If he is innocent (that is morally innocent by reason of insanity which can be demonstrated to be congenital, inherent, or of irresistible force), he will at once be acquitted.

Actually, the statement was the epitome of sanctimony, for the *Times,* along with virtually everyone else in England at the time, cried out for the blood of Daniel McNaughton.

The most thoughtful statement came from the 24-year-old Queen. When she heard of Drummond's death she said, "The proofs of the wretch McNaughton's madness seem to the Queen very slight, and indeed, there is and should be a difference between that madness which is such that a man knows not what he does, and madness which does not prevent a man from purposely buying pistols, and then with determined purpose watching and shooting a person."

A highly appropriate statement, even today.

The inquest was a routine affair. It took place on January 26, 1843 at the Lion and Goat Tavern on Grosvenor Street, near the residence of the deceased. Mr. Gell, the coroner for Westminster, and the jury dutifully filed through the Drummond house to view the mortal remains, and then retired for the hearing. They found that Edward Drummond, aged fifty, late secretary to the Prime Minister, died as a result of "willful murder" at the hands of Daniel McNaughton.

Now that the dead man was officially declared a victim of murder, the public was assured of a sensational trial in the very near future. All the necessary ingredients were present: a shocking crime, a state of general outrage over the nature of the crime, and a growing controversy as to whether or not the slayer was sane. McNaughton's sanity became the focal point for a chauvinistic, literary duel between the London and Glasgow papers. While the London press made every effort to prove McNaughton a sane, rational murderer, the Glasgow journalists set out to prove that their native son was obviously insane, and therefore not guilty of murder.

Meanwhile, on Saturday, January 28, McNaughton was committed to Newgate prison to await trial. On the same day an advertisement appeared in the form of a letter to the *Times* asserting that if the late, unfortunate Mr. Drummond had only taken Morison & Moat's Universal Medicine, after having been so grievously wounded, he would still be alive.

Thrust by Drummond's death before the harsh scrutiny

of the press, McNaughton's life became an open book. He was born in Glasgow, the illegitimate son of a respectable wood turner, who not only gave the boy his name, but raised him and taught him a trade as well. There was apparently no friction between them, for after his apprenticeship, young Daniel remained with his father for five years as a journeyman. During that period he had been, according to his father's testimony, "A steady worker and a kind son."

He was a quiet young man who spent much of his spare time reading romantic novels and plays. Perhaps this was what inspired him to leave home and join a troupe of strolling players. If there was one thing that Daniel McNaughton liked, however, it was money, and the life of an actor did not provide him with enough of it. Before long he had settled down to earning a living at the trade he knew best—wood turning. He proved to be a canny businessman, a trait that was coupled with a propensity for hard work. This unbeatable combination soon made him a relatively affluent young man. His hours were long, often he slept in his shop, and he became frugal to the point of parsimony. He cooked his own food in the shop, dressed poorly, and watched each penny as if it were his last. Most of his reading matter was borrowed, and when he incurred fines at the library, he always managed to talk his way out of paying.

Those who knew McNaughton insisted that while living in Scotland he was quiet, retiring, and kindly, in spite of his stinginess. His interests were largely in intellectual subjects. He tried his hand at composing poetry and acrostics, which were considered neither bad nor brilliant. He was a member of the Glasgow Mechanics Institute, where he attended lectures on anatomy, physiology, and

natural philosophy. He did, however, have certain peculiarities which were noticed by others. During the six or
seven years that he was in business for himself, he moved
his shop and his lodgings frequently. Occasionally, for no
apparent reason, he was known to throw chips of wood
at customers who were leaving his shop, but this was
attributed to a spirit of fun rather than anything else.
Fellow Glasgow lodgers who had shared rooms with him
related how McNaughton often cried out in his sleep, or
would walk about at night uttering such exclamations as,
"By Jove!" or "My God!" Usually, said informants, these
epithets were followed by spasmodic unconnected sentences. There were other stories of strange behavior on
his part. He was known to bathe regularly in the river
every morning, even on the bitterest of cold winter days,
and when he suffered from one of his frequent headaches, he would run from the house, clutching his forehead, and rush to the banks of the Clyde, where he would
dunk his head in the water. Such actions were not regarded as too strange, though, for Daniel McNaughton
had acquired quite a reputation as a hypochondriac. (Hy-
pochondria is regarded today by psychiatrists as a common
symptom among psychotic patients.)

The *Glasgow Constitutional* referred to McNaughton as
"a radical in politics, and inclined to infidelity in religion."
He apparently did not have any specific sectarian lean-
ings, although he did attend religious services occasionally.
On the subject of politics, however, he was quite vociferous.
Although he did not always take sides, he argued frequently and loudly for and against specific issues which
aroused his interest. His opinions of various statesmen
were reported to be generally intelligent and thoughtful.
The *Times* of London suggested that he was "tolerably

sane" on all subjects save that of the Tories. The newspaper even suggested somewhat facetiously that McNaughton had probably killed Drummond purposely, feeling that he had done the country a service merely by eliminating a single member of the conservative faction.

It was not until 1841 that McNaughton began to behave in a noticeably irrational manner. Having grown increasingly restless, he took to wandering frequently about the countryside when he should have been attending to business. Such unseemly conduct did not suit the frugal, industrious young Scottish tradesman. Friends and acquaintances looked askance at it. They did not yet know that these excursions were early attempts to escape from imaginary enemies. Before long Daniel McNaughton made no secret of the "fact" that he was being followed everywhere by spies. He said that they laughed at him, insulted him, and accused him of crimes. When he told his father about these elusive persecutors, the elder McNaughton offered to accompany him in order to see what they looked like, but he was told, "That will be of no use; if they see you they will not follow me at all."

Hoping to obtain protection from his chimerical enemies, he went to see Sir James Campbell, Lord Provost of Glasgow and superintendent of police. He told Campbell that he was being incessantly hounded by "certain parties" who bore him ill will, that they shook their umbrellas and walking sticks at him, that they threatened him with their fists, and made his life intolerable. One man, he declared, followed him everywhere and threw straws at him, which, he added, were symbolic of the concerted effort being made to reduce him to beggary.

"They forced me to flee from my home by their machinations!" he told Campbell excitedly. "I had to flee to the suburbs to escape them."

He was becoming more and more disturbed. Mrs. Patterson, his landlady, said that while he had lodged with her he had appeared increasingly frightened. From time to time, she said, McNaughton was seized with "some kind of a fit," when he attacked furniture and broke dishes. Furthermore, during the night he could be heard moaning and groaning. The poor woman became genuinely alarmed when he told her that "Devils" in human form were seeking to murder him, and that if they did not leave him alone he would take pistols and "blow their heads off."

Tormented nearly out of his wits, McNaughton complained that he was unable to sleep. Friends and acquaintances recalled that he had become pale and thin. Again and again he went back to the police, pleading pitifully with them to protect him from his persecutors. Each time they were polite, but they insisted that they could do nothing for him without tangible proof. In desperation he contacted Alexander Johnstone, a member of Parliament. Expressing his fears, he asked the M.P. for advice and protection. Johnstone recommended the police, but McNaughton was insistent, explaining that they were of no help. He kept after Johnstone for almost a year, either calling at his office in Glasgow or writing to him in London. The harassed M.P. finally wrote McNaughton and said, "I am very sorry I can do nothing for you. You are labouring under a delusion of the mind, there is no reason for your entertaining such fears."

He had gone everywhere for help, but no matter which way Daniel McNaughton turned, he found himself surrounded by enemies who sought to degrade and destroy him. He was caught in the grip of a mounting terror that forced him to choose between two extreme alternatives: fight or flight. Desiring only peace of mind he chose what seemed to be the simpler and more practical choice—flight. Explaining that he was the victim of a conspiracy, he sold his business to a William Carlow for £1,000 and hastily departed from Glasgow. Certainly, he reasoned, the Tories would not torment him in Europe, so with only the fervent desire for tranquillity, he fled to the Continent.

Unfortunately McNaughton was unable to find what he had sought. Pursued as he was by a delusion that was becoming increasingly systematized, he found himself no less tortured by his persecutors in France and Holland than he had been in Glasgow. Every Parisian wearing a cape was a potential assassin seeking his life. The sound of each footstep behind him belonged to one of the legions of enemies who now hounded him night and day. To venture near the banks of the Seine after dark was to risk death, to cross a footbridge over an Amsterdam canal was to court disaster. In every shadowy doorway lurked a foe who sought his life. It became impossible to elude them, the flight had been useless. In order to protect himself he was left with only one alternative—to fight.

In paranoid delusions such as the one that gripped Daniel McNaughton, it is common for the sufferer to single out a particular individual as his chief persecutor. Since the most prominent Tory of the day was Sir Robert Peel, it was only logical to McNaughton that the Prime Minister was responsible for his sufferings. There was no longer any need to be afraid. All that stood between himself and peace was one man, and if that man could be got rid of, all would be well again. Having decided on a definite course of action, McNaughton returned to his native Scotland.

He had to proceed cautiously in order to elude his

pursuers, so taking the most circuitous route he could devise, McNaughton went as quickly as possible to the town of Paisley, just outside Glasgow. Looking over his shoulder often, and ducking from time to time into doorways and *culs de sac,* he finally made his way to the shop of Alexander Martin, a gunsmith. There he purchased a pair of pistols, a powder horn, a supply of percussion caps, and some newly cast balls. He would have preferred a pair of matched guns, had they been available, but time was now of the essence, and he could not afford to wait for the gunsmith to fashion a mate to the weapon he favored. It was absolutely essential to the success of his undertaking that he have two pistols, for if he missed the first time, he would have a second loaded, primed, and ready for the *coup de grâce.* In 1843, an assassin with only one pistol had no second chance in the event of a misfire, and Daniel McNaughton, well aware that he was an amateur, wished to leave nothing to chance. As soon as he had transacted his business with Martin, he checked the time and hurried to the railway station. There was just enough time to catch the last train to London, where, within a few weeks, he was to cross the chasm between obscurity and notoriety. It was an ironic destiny that awaited Daniel McNaughton. Little did he dream that the crime he was about to commit would earn him a tragic immortality.

The trial began on Friday, March 3, 1843. Every avenue to the court was crowded with well-dressed men and women who had flocked to see the most celebrated courtroom drama of the day. Among the distinguished spectators were the American and Belgian Ministers to Great Britain. Both houses of Parliament were liberally represented and, virtually unnoticed by the public, seated just to the right of the judges, was Prince Albert, royal consort to Her Majesty, the Queen.

It appeared quite obvious that the prosecution felt it had a simple, uncomplicated case, for Solicitor-General Waddington had only one colleague to assist him. The defense, on the other hand, clearly expected an uphill battle, for appearing on McNaughton's behalf was no less a person than the Queen's Counsel, Henry Thomas, later Lord Cockburn, one of England's most distinguished lawyers, with three associates.

The first excitement to erupt in the courtroom came immediately after the prisoner answered "Not guilty" to the Lord Chief Justice's question, "How do you plead?"

There arose such a commotion that the judge had to rap his gavel repeatedly for order. When quiet was finally restored, Cockburn stood up and qualified his client's plea, "Not guilty by reason of insanity." Once again the loud murmuring of excited voices disturbed the decorum of the courtroom and again it was necessary for the Lord Chief Justice to pound his gavel until silence was restored. During the entire disorder McNaughton himself sat motionless in the dock with his head thrown back as though he were asleep, or in a trance, an attitude he maintained until the first witnesses were called to the bar.

The prosecution's opening remarks were nothing more than a rehash of the crime, coupled with an emotional eulogy of the late Edward Drummond, an obvious attempt to gain the sympathy of the jury. Very cleverly, prosecutor Waddington made it plain that the defense would attempt in every way to validate its plea of insanity. He added that all persons who made attempts on the lives of prominent people were under a mental strain, but that they nevertheless had to be held accountable for their actions.

"If," said the prosecutor, "you believe that when he fired the pistol he was incapable of distinguishing between right and wrong,—if you believe he was under the influence and control of some disease of the mind which prevented him from being conscious that he was committing a crime . . . he is entitled to your acquittal, but it is my duty . . . to tell you that nothing short of that excuse can excuse him upon the principle of English law."

It had now become clear that the trial taking place was much more than an ordinary murder case. The prisoner had admitted the killing. It was a historic hearing which had to determine whether or not Daniel McNaughton was insane, but also, and more important for the future, had to establish a new definition of insanity in the legal sense.

On the basis of previous cases, the solicitor-general insisted that McNaughton be found guilty as charged, and on that basis alone the jury would have had to bring in a verdict of guilty. All the cases Waddington cited concerned persons who had been plainly suffering from varying degrees of mental illness, who had been convicted solely because juries had not considered them afflicted with a "total permanent or temporary want of reason." What made this argument particularly effective at the time was that any non-medical person in the courtroom would have considered Daniel McNaughton more rational than any of those previously executed "madmen." Yet each of them had been found sane enough by English justice to face the death penalty. After dwelling at length on the precedent-setting cases of insanity and the law, the prosecutor enjoined the jury to serve only the cause of justice. His remarks were so objective that it is hard to judge over a century and a quarter later whether his attitude stemmed from a high degree of confidence, or the superior ethics of a more dignified era.

The balance of the trial itself was, as expected, sensational and highly charged with human drama. One of the ironies of the case was that most of the witnesses who knew McNaughton personally strenuously rejected any suggestion that they might have thought him insane, because they thought such allegations might injure his character. Expert medical testimony, however, was overwhelmingly on the side of the defense. Dr. Munro, the chief medical witness, who was director of Bethlem Royal Hospital (Bedlam), concluded his testimony by saying, "It is my decided opinion that the prisoner is laboring under insanity. I have not the slightest doubt of it. A man may be perfectly insane on one point, though thoroughly sane on another." But from the standpoint of wording, the testimony of Dr. McMurdo, the surgeon of Newgate prison, is particularly interesting, especially in view of the "irresistible impulse" defense so widely used today. McNaughton, said McMurdo, ". . . was decidedly insane upon the subject of persecution, and the act he committed was the result of an impulse over which he had no control."

What occurred next had never happened in any courtroom. The weight of such massive medical testimony was so great that the prosecutor was unable to refute a word of it. In a precedent-shattering address, he told the jury that he could not think of asking them for a verdict against the prisoner. However, he assured them, whatever their verdict might be, the ends of justice would be served—and indeed they were. Not only did the jury decline to have the Lord Chief Justice sum up the evidence for them, they did not even leave the courtroom. After turning around in the jury box for about two minutes, they returned their historic verdict: "Acquittal, on the grounds of insanity."

The unexpected outcome of McNaughton's trial produced a violent public reaction. On the following Monday, March 6, 1843, a *Times* editorial said in part:

> It is neither our duty nor our wish to cavil at the verdict of the jury. They doubtless performed their part conscientiously enough. We only want to know for the benefit of simple folks what in the future is to be considered sanity? It appears that it is not enough that a man should talk and write correctly on matters of business, give a good account of what is passing around him, or pronounce a correct opinion of men and measures, in order to be considered sane, but if he cherish the fancies of a diseased imagination, this is sufficient to obtain for him the character of a monomaniac; and if he only proceeds to commit murder, that is the climax of his monomania . . .

The readers had no intention of being outshouted, as it were, by professional journalists. On March 7, a letter to the editors appeared which said:

> I have in contemplation the accomplishment of a certain pet project, which unfortunately involves some degree of violence in its attainment; I mean however, to retain beforehand some of the most eminent medical men of the day as witnesses of my monomaniacal possession [in order to] reward my perseverance with a comfortable and permanent abode in Bethlem Hospital at the expense of the nation.
>
> Your very insane servant,
> PRO HOC VICE

The apogee of public ire was reached on March 8 when the *Times* published a poem entitled *On A Late Acquittal,* by a reader who called himself simply T. Campbell:

Ye people of England! Exult and be glad
For ye're now at the will of the merciless mad.
Why ye say that but three authorities reign—
Crown, Commons, and Lords!—You omit the insane!
They're a privileged class, whom no statute controls,
And their murderous charter exists in their souls.
Do they wish to spill blood—they have only to play
A few pranks—get asylum'd a month and a day—
Then heigh! To escape from the mad-doctor's keys,
And to pistol and stab whomever they please.
Now the dog has a human-like wit in creation,
He resembles most nearly our own generation.
Then if madmen for murder escape with impunity,
Why deny a poor dog the same noble immunity!
So, if a dog or man bite you, beware being nettled;
For crime is no crime—when the mind is unsettled.

As the torrent of unfavorable comment continued to appear in the press, a heated debate took place in the House of Lords, on Monday, March 13, 1843. They acknowledged that to hang an insane man was tantamount to murder, yet, like the public, they disapproved of the court's verdict. The law was clear to these noble gentlemen, the McNaughton decision was not.

One of the last news items concerning Daniel McNaughton appeared in a weekly paper, *The Atlas,* on Saturday, March 18. It said:

> On Monday this wretched criminal was removed from Newgate to Bethlehem [Bethlem] Hospital. McNaughton received with evident satisfaction the instruction that he was to leave Newgate, and walked with a quick, firm step to the outer prison gate where a cabriolet was in waiting to receive him.

Obviously, society was not yet ready to look dispassionately at mental illness—especially when it precipitated assassination. Certainly, twenty-two years later, the American public would have reacted in quite the same way the British did, had another psychotic assassin, John Wilkes Booth, similarly been tried and acquitted. Booth, however, hit his mark, Abraham Lincoln. Would he have escaped the gallows on grounds of insanity, had he lived to stand trial? Psychotic or not, he figured in an incredible conspiracy, a conspiracy that succeeded. But other questions arise. Would McNaughton have been acquitted had he succeeded in assassinating Sir Robert Peel? What would have happened in 1963, had Lee Harvey Oswald lived to stand trial? And suppose he had been tried and found not guilty by reason of insanity? Would twentieth-century Americans have reacted any differently from the English of 1843?

It is a peculiar twist of fate that as John Wilkes Booth lay hiding in a Virginia swamp, Daniel McNaughton was slowly expiring in Broadmoor Hospital, to which he had been transferred from Bethlem. He survived Booth by only seven days, dying quietly in bed, a forgotten, middle-aged "lunatic," and as such was not dignified by an obituary notice, not even in the papers which had clamored so vehemently for his blood. For he had long since been transformed from a human being into a few lines of legalistic jargon.

6

DISSECTION
of a CONSPIRACY

Before he died in 1926, Robert Todd Lincoln, the only surviving son of Abraham Lincoln, burned an undetermined quantity of his father's personal papers. A friend came to visit him at the time, and expressed horror at the sight of such historically vital documents going up in smoke. Mr. Lincoln explained that the papers he was destroying contained documentary evidence that a member of his father's cabinet had been guilty of treason, and he felt that such scandal was best deleted from historical records. This was a strong accusation but, considering the source, it must still carry a great deal of weight. Happily for posterity Mr. Lincoln was persuaded to permit the remaining papers to be placed in the Library of Congress where they were kept sealed from public view until 1947. When they were opened, nothing was found to confirm the friend's statement. It seemed, therefore, that either the incriminating documents had been destroyed, or the story was untrue. Years of painstaking historical detective work and unexpected recent discoveries, however, seem to indicate that Robert Todd Lincoln's disclosure of treason by one of his father's cabinet members was highly understated. On the basis of the evidence—circumstantial though much of it may be—there is every reason to believe that Abraham Lincoln was indeed the victim of an extensive conspiracy, and that the dominant figure was not John Wilkes Booth, but Edwin M. Stanton, Lincoln's dictatorial Secretary of War.

Because Abraham Lincoln has been virtually canonized since his murder on Good Friday of 1865, people tend to forget that he was one of the most hated men ever to enter the White House. There was so much sentiment against him that even before he left Springfield, Illinois to take office in Washington there were threats against his life. The state of the Union on the eve of his oath of office was chaotic. Secessionist feeling was sweeping the South like a plague, and vituperative mail addressed to Lincoln had reached alarming proportions. In *The War Years,* Carl Sandburg cited an extreme example: a letter from Fillmore, Louisiana, in which the infuriated writer used the phrase "God-damned" twenty-two times in one paragraph.

Detective Allan Pinkerton foiled the first major assassination attempt in Maryland. There, a gang of violently pro-South conspirators had planned to kill the President-elect when the inaugural train pulled into Baltimore. The plot was foiled by having Lincoln change trains at the last minute in Philadelphia, disguising him, and secretly smuggling him into the capital under heavy escort on the morning of February 23, 1861. Subsequently there were other Presidential assassination plots, most of which were hatched in the heart of the Confederacy. They ranged from kidnap-ambushes to a bizarre attempt by a woman wearing a heavy black veil who actually kissed Lincoln in an effort to infect him with smallpox.

We are concerned here, however, with the conspiracy that culminated in Ford's Theater when John Wilkes Booth fired the fatal bullet on the night of April 14, 1865.

A Marylander by birth, Booth was fervently devoted to the Confederate cause, but instead of joining the rebel army he took advantage of his position as a famous actor to engage in an assortment of undercover activities on behalf of the South. When it became obvious to him in 1864 that a Union victory was inevitable, he hatched a wild scheme to kidnap Lincoln, spirit him away to Richmond, and turn him over to the Confederates. This, he reckoned, would turn the tide and enable the Confederacy to dictate a peace. Failing that, he conceived of offering the President's safe return in exchange for one hundred thousand rebel prisoners, thereby making it possible for the South to revitalize its armed forces and continue the war.

To successfully accomplish such a bold deed, Booth required accomplices. First there was twenty-one-year-old John Harrison Surratt, Jr., a Maryland-born Confederate spy and underground courier. He was an ex-divinity student with a talent for remaining anonymous, outwardly inoffensive, and closemouthed. It was through Surratt that his mother's Washington boarding house at 541 H Street N.W. became the central meeting place for Booth and his immediate circle of conspirators. (The house still stands today, somewhat altered physically, and now numbered 604.)

Next there was David E. Herold, twenty-three. A one-time drugstore clerk, Herold was also a Marylander, the problem child of his family, partially because he had been alternately spoiled, bullied, and pampered by seven older sisters. He fell under Booth's spell as a fan, and became the actor's willing accomplice for any endeavor after his offer of friendship was readily accepted and reciprocated. Booth's interest in Herold was purely calculated. The youth's chief passion was quail hunting, and he knew the Maryland countryside as well as anyone alive. His value to a conspiracy involving the abduction of the President was obvious.

The most unlikely of the conspirators was George Andrew Atzerodt, thirty-three. An illiterate Prussian immigrant, he worked as a carriage painter in Port Tobacco, Virginia, and picked up side money during the war as a boatman for the Confederate underground. It was in this latter capacity that Booth intended to use him. But he was a man so lacking in worthwhile attributes—especially courage—that it has been suggested he was chosen for a secondary reason, as a human bone to be tossed to the inevitable pursuers, while the rest of the conspirators got away. This is pure conjecture, of course.

Samuel Bland Arnold, twenty-eight, was an ex-Confederate soldier and boyhood friend of Booth. A resident of Baltimore, he was drawn into the plot at the same time as another old friend of the past, twenty-seven-year-old Michael O'Laughlin, who had also served in the Confederate army. Their part in the abduction scheme was to smuggle a trunkload of firearms, ammunition, knives, and handcuffs into Washington to be used in the kidnapping.

Of all the conspirators, Lewis Paine, twenty, was the most dangerous. A brooding, hulking six-footer of enormous physical strength, he was born Lewis Thornton

Powell in Alabama, and raised on the hellfire and damnation backwoods sermons of his preacher father. A Confederate parolee, veteran of the Peninsular campaign, the bloody battles of Antietam, Chancellorsville, and Pickett's charge at Gettysburg, he was fearless, embittered, and filled with nearly paranoid hatred for Northerners, especially Abraham Lincoln. (He once bragged that before battles he had drunk toasts to victory from the skulls of dead Yankees.) Though he had a number of aliases, he preferred to use the name Paine. Like David Herold, he first met Booth as an admiring fan.

Paine's most significant meeting with John Wilkes Booth, however, took place early in February 1865 in Baltimore, where the actor had gone for a hurried conference with Arnold and O'Laughlin. It was a chance meeting on the street in front of Barnum's Hotel. Booth recognized Paine as the admiring giant who had offered him such enthusiastic praise after a performance not long before in Richmond. He invited Paine for a drink, and learned of his fanatical hatreds. Recognizing a valuable accomplice in the youth, Booth recruited him into the band of conspirators.

Three other persons were also eventually tried for the murder of Abraham Lincoln: Mary E. Surratt, proprietress of the boarding house on H Street; Dr. Samuel A. Mudd, of Bryantown, Maryland; and Edward Spangler, a coarse and shabby alcoholic, employed as a stagehand at Ford's Theater. Of Mary Surratt, more will be said later. As for Dr. Mudd, in all probability his only complicity was the introduction of Booth to John Surratt and attending the actor's broken leg after the assassination. Spangler had procured eighty-one feet of rope to be used in the earlier kidnapping plot and cared for Booth's horse on the night of April 14 while the play was in progress.

But back to Paine. Shortly after the Baltimore meeting
with Booth, he rang the doorbell of Mrs. Surratt's house
and identified himself as Mr. Wood. He wore a thread-
bare black overcoat and asked for John Surratt. On being
told that Surratt was not there, Paine asked for the young
man's mother, who came, admitted him, and fed him a
hearty meal upon hearing that he hadn't eaten all day.
The man who admitted Paine, and supplied the above
information, was a boarder of Mrs. Surratt's, Louis Wiechmann, a clerk in the War Department, and later principal
government witness against his landlady (see Document
II).

Wiechmann, described by Jim Bishop in *The Day Lincoln Was Shot* as "big and soft and pungent . . . drawn
to eavesdropping and gossip," soon recognized that something suspicious was going on in the house on H Street.
He observed the comings and goings of Booth and the
other conspirators, he noted that they met together for
strange conferences at odd hours of the night, and frequently were armed. Accordingly, Wiechmann reported
his suspicions to Captain D.H.L. Gleason of the War
Department, giving the name and description of every
person involved. Years later, previously classified War
Department documents revealed that Stanton was fully
aware as early as January 1865 of the plot's existence
and the identities of the conspirators. *Yet, no action was
taken.*

The surrender of General Robert E. Lee on April 9,
1865 made the kidnapping of Lincoln useless. But the plot
had failed before this because of last-minute changes of
plans on the part of the President. There is, however,
some evidence to indicate that after the kidnapping scheme
misfired, Booth persuaded Paine to ambush and assassinate
Lincoln some time after March 20, the original target

date of the kidnapping. The idea to assassinate must have originated after an alternate abduction scheme collapsed shortly before Lee's surrender. There is ample reason to question whether the idea was born in Booth's mind or planted there by some unknown person. The only one of the conspirators to display any good sense at this point was Samuel Arnold, who wrote Booth a letter urging him to drop the idea of any assault on the person of the President, and to use his head before doing anything rash. Had Arnold said nothing his name would never have come up and his participation in the conspiracy might never have been known.

In any event, after Lee's surrender Booth had only one idea in mind: to assassinate Lincoln. This is not conjecture. After his capture Paine told his interrogators that he and Booth had gone to the White House grounds on the night of April 10 to hear the President's victory speech. He quoted Booth as snarling afterwards, "That is the last speech *he* will ever make!" And in view of the fact that Paine hardly possessed sufficient intellectual capacity to lie, he probably told the truth.

If Lincoln's speech infuriated Booth (it has been suggested that he was angered by the President's recommendation that certain Negroes be given the vote), there were many men on the Union side who were outraged for other reasons. Radical Republicans favoring a hard-line post-war policy must have regarded the address with alarm. A harsh policy toward the defeated South, if handled carefully, could reduce the former Confederacy to the status of a colony that could be plundered, exploited, and kept in perpetual subjugation. The chief advocate of such a policy was Secretary of War Edwin M. Stanton.

Since Stanton knew all about Booth's unsuccessful kidnap plot, including the *dramatis personae,* he could easily have taken steps to prevent them from accomplishing anything further. Simple harassment would have sufficed. As the highest government official charged with the personal security of the President, Stanton could have ensured that security with little or no difficulty. But, as we shall see, he did nothing of the sort.

Lincoln's plans to attend the performance of *Our American Cousin* at Ford's Theater on April 14, 1865 were well known. He had invited General and Mrs. Grant to attend with him, but they had declined at the urging of Grant's superior, the Secretary of War. Stanton was also invited to attend with the Presidential party, but he, too, turned down the invitation.

The folklore of the land is most explicit about Lincoln's premonitions of death. But there is nothing folkloristic about the fact that the President specifically expressed concern about his personal safety that night. There are ample records in existence to verify that whenever he felt the need for special protection he requested it. On the afternoon of April 14 Abraham Lincoln made a personal trip to the War Department, went directly to Stanton, and requested the presence of Major Thomas L. Eckert as personal bodyguard that night. Major Eckert was a man of great strength, whom Lincoln had seen break five pokers in succession over one arm.

Witness to what happened that day was William Crook, a White House guard, who wrote later that Lincoln had said to him on the way to Stanton's office, "Crook, do you know, I believe there are men who want to take my life. And I have no doubt that they will do it." Crook tried to dissuade the President from making such statements, but Lincoln persisted, saying, "Other men have been assassinated. I have perfect confidence in those who are around me. In every one of you men. I know no one could do it and escape alive. But if it is to be done, it is impossible to prevent it."

Difficult as it may be to believe, when Lincoln requested that Major Eckert serve as his bodyguard that night, Stanton refused on the ground that the major had urgent telegraphic duties to perform at the War Department. Incredulity turns to suspicion when we learn that despite this bold-faced refusal of the President's request, Stanton did not keep Eckert on duty that evening. Eckert went home at dinner-time and never returned to the office. Subsequent historical research also revealed that there were no urgent telegraph messages received or sent that night.

Had General Grant and Stanton accompanied the Lincolns to the theater there would have been a heavy military escort. But there was none. In place of Major Eckert, a Major Henry Rathbone and his fiancée accompanied the President (see Document III). Major Rathbone was a competent staff officer attached to the War Department, but he was not a man of great strength, and though he grappled with Booth after the President was shot, he was not able to prevent his escape. Assigned to guard the Presidential box from outside was John F. Parker of the Metropolitan Police Force.

Examination of Parker's record raises the question how he ever managed to keep his job, let alone draw the important assignment of guarding the President. In addition to being a chronic drunkard, Parker had frequently been reprimanded for drinking on duty, loafing on his beat, sleeping on duty, and insubordinate behavior. Furthermore, he had been in trouble for bullying street-walkers, using foul language, insulting ladies, and once for firing his revolver through the window of a brothel while drunk. On April 14, 1865 his behavior was true to form. Instead of remaining at his post, he left the Presidential box unguarded and went to a saloon. He was not seen until the next day when he showed up at Police Headquarters. Incredible as it seems, Parker was not dismissed.

The assassination itself was badly bungled. Although Booth succeeded in shooting Lincoln, he broke his leg while leaping to the stage prior to his getaway. Paine successfully forced his way into the house of Secretary of State William H. Seward, who was in bed with a fractured jaw. After brutally attacking Seward's son Frederick, the wild-eyed giant pulled a bowie knife and threw himself at the bedridden Secretary, slashing, cursing, and stabbing. He was promptly counterattacked by two members of the household, whereupon he wrenched free, charged down the stairs covered with blood, bellowing, "I'm mad! I'm mad!" and got away. Seward miraculously escaped serious injury because a surgical brace he was wearing at the time deflected Paine's knife. Frederick Seward, too, was only superficially wounded.

While this was happening, Herold made good his exit from Washington to rendezvous with Booth at a prearranged spot across the river in Maryland. Atzerodt had been given the assignment of killing Andrew Johnson, but it is not surprising that he failed to do so. He was hardly the man to carry out a task requiring such nerve. He had gone so far as to check into the Kirkwood House, where Johnson was staying, and had kept an uneasy watch on the Vice President.

One of the strangest sidelights to the assassination is that John Wilkes Booth paid a visit to Johnson on the afternoon of April 14 while the latter was meeting with the President at the White House. The calling card with Booth's name on it stuck like a thorn in Andrew Johnson's side for the rest of his life. There was never any explanation as to why Booth had come to see him, and Johnson's political enemies made it a point to draw dark inferences from the call. Perhaps it was nothing more than a red herring, planted purposely by Booth for that exact reason. No one will ever know.

The truth of what actually happened before, during, and after the assassination of Abraham Lincoln is obscured by a staggering mass of information, misinformation, lies, and contradictions. What emerges from this twisted tangle of statements numbs the imagination. Booth and Herold escaped from Washington and eluded their pursuers in the swamps and thickets of Maryland until the night of April 25, nearly ten days after the murder, when they were cornered in the burning barn of farmer Garrett near Bowling Green, Virginia. On April 16 Mrs. Mary Surratt, Lewis Paine, Michael O'Laughlin, Samuel B. Arnold, and Edward Spangler were arrested. For reasons that are still unclear, John Harrison Surratt was permitted to escape from the United States, and George Atzerodt was not arrested until April 21. Dr. Samuel Mudd was arrested on April 22, and charged with being part of the conspiracy. A number of others who were known (and who later admitted) to have aided Booth and Herold during their flight were not arrested.

Armed with facts readily available today (presented and documented especially well in Theodore Roscoe's *The Web of Conspiracy*),[1] it is difficult not to conclude that Edwin M. Stanton himself was at the center of it all, pulling strings from his high position like a relentless puppet master bent on changing the destiny of the nation according to his own will.

The trial was conducted by a military tribunal that may very well have been unconstitutional because, technically, such a court has jurisdiction only over military personnel, and in this case, all the defendants were civilians. But the mood of the nation was vengeful; even former Confederates were shocked. And the court was convened to convict. The government trotted out a series of witnesses, a number of whom proved later to be liars, convicted criminals, and former Confederate spies, but whose testimony helped to ensure the convictions. Of the eight persons tried, four were condemned to the gallows: Paine, Herold, Atzerodt, and Mary Surratt. There was no question about the guilt of Paine and Herold. Atzerodt, the grubby little man with the haunted eyes, was a cowardly fool, and a minor accomplice, but he hardly deserved to hang. As for Mary Surratt, there was reasonable doubt as to her guilt. Theodore Roscoe asserts, "By and large, history's consensus is that Mrs. Surratt was not guilty as charged." Of the other defendants, Dr. Mudd, Arnold, and O'Laughlin were given life sentences, and Spangler got six years.

Even after the executions, however, entirely too many unanswered questions remained. At the trial David Herold testified that Booth had told him of the existence of thirty-five persons in the conspiracy. This information was especially interesting in view of the fact that after Booth's death, his diary was removed from a coat pocket and turned over to Lt. Colonel Everton Conger, who personally took it to Washington and gave it to Colonel (later

General) Lafayette C. Baker, head of the Secret Service. Baker in turn gave the diary to his chief, Stanton, who later testified that he had read all the entries carefully. Three men are known to have read the diary: Conger, Baker, and Stanton. *Yet the diary was not introduced as evidence at the conspirators' trial.* Why? Furthermore, in 1867, after publication of Baker's *History of the U.S. Secret Service,*[2] a furor arose in Congress because his book stated that such a diary existed. Both houses clamored to examine it. When it was finally resurrected from an obscure War Department file, eighteen pages were missing, carefully cut out. The missing pages covered the period leading up to the night that Lincoln was assassinated. Could these possibly have contained details about the thirty-five unnamed conspirators alluded to in Herold's testimony?

The implications are serious. Baker claimed that when he gave the diary to Stanton it was intact. Stanton later asserted that the eighteen pages were already missing when he received the book. If Conger said anything at all, there is no record of his statement. Someone had to be lying. Here, again, the finger points to Stanton, because he did go on record as having examined "all the entries" in the diary with great care.

More facts seem to cast a shadow of guilt over Stanton. His stage-management of the conspirators' capture was peculiarly inept for a man who not only knew who each of them was, but who had so recently administered a successful war. Suspicion increases even more in light of certain events that followed the assassination. All telegraph lines out of Washington *except* Stanton's military line were cut immediately after the crime. No explanation has ever been given for this. The news of the assassina-

tion was thus delayed outside of the capital, thereby giving
Stanton's picked team of pursuers an advantage over outsiders. Atzerodt was not picked up on the night of the
shooting, though he made little effort to cover his tracks.
Booth, who might have provided the answers to missing
questions, was shot when every effort should have been
made to take him alive. Although the mortally wounded
assassin lingered until about 7:00 A.M.—about five hours
after being taken from the burning barn—no effort was
made to interrogate him, and the various versions of what
actually happened are so different that it is impossible
to determine which one was true.

The military tribunal that conducted the trial was a
creation of Stanton's, and it was he who selected the
generals who served on it. A contemporary writer, George
Alfred Townsend, described it this way:

> Excepting Judge Holt [Judge Advocate General Joseph Holt],
> the court has shown as little ability as could be expected from
> soldiers, placed in unenviable publicity, and upon a duty for
> which they are disqualified, both by education and acumen.
> Witness the lack of dignity in Hunter [Major General David
> Hunter], who opened the court by a coarse allusion to "Humbug
> chivalry"; of Lew Wallace [author of *Ben Hur*], whose heat and
> intolerance were appropriately urged in the most exceptional
> English; of Howe [Brigadier General Alvin P. Howe], whose
> tirade against the rebel general Johnson was feeble as it was un-
> generous! This court was needed to show us at least the petty
> tyranny of martial law and the pettiness of martial justice.[3]

It was Stanton who drafted the conspirators' indictment
so that, in addition to the defendants in court, Jefferson
Davis and the entire Confederacy were indicted by im-
plication. It was Stanton who blocked the court's intention
to save Mary Surratt from the gallows. Although she was

found guilty, despite the element of reasonable doubt that would have set her free in a civilian court, the tribunal did not vote unanimously to give her a death sentence. A deal was made by which they would so vote in return for an understanding that a clemency petition would be forwarded immediately to President Johnson, asking for a commutation of her sentence to life imprisonment. Although a number of petitioners, including priests, lawyers, and other prominent persons, went directly to the White House, they were turned away by two senators, staunch Stanton supporters, both of whom, strangely enough, committed suicide shortly afterward. Even Judge Holt, one of the three "conductors" of the trial, who had argued for Mrs. Surratt's life, was unable to get the tribunal's petition to the President. It was also Stanton who later instigated impeachment proceedings against Andrew Johnson.

Whether Edwin McMasters Stanton engineered an assassination plot, manipulated another man's plot from the sidelines, or did nothing but permit a plot to reach its inevitable conclusion makes no difference now. Whatever the case, he, along with a number of other radical Republicans, had ample reason to want Abraham Lincoln and his conciliatory post-war policies out of the way, a point touched upon earlier, and one which demands some amplification. Whereas Lincoln favored amnesty, reconciliation, and true reunion, Stanton had other ideas. His plan, which had some support in Congress and in the industrial community, was to deprive the former Confederate states of their statehood and to reclassify them as territories. He proposed that their legislatures be abolished, that they be administered by military governors responsible to the War Department, and of course that they have no consequential representation in Congress. The South would thus be effectively crushed, its people disenfranchised, without hope of ever being anything more than dwellers in a colonial appendage to the industrial North.

The fact that Andrew Johnson did not knuckle under to pressures, could not be impeached, and did his best to carry on with Abraham Lincoln's policies, prevented Stanton and his supporters from imposing such a fate on the South. If this was the crux of the conspiracy, then it failed miserably. As for the conspiracy itself, there are still a number of unanswered questions. Why were none of the key individuals arrested on the night of the murder? Why was neither Booth's mistress nor his fiancée interrogated? Why were so many witnesses who could have shed much light on the case never called to testify at the trial? Who were the thirty-five men alluded to by David Herold? Why was there so much confusion surrounding the body of John Wilkes Booth? Indeed, this last question gained such momentum that by the turn of the century there were serious doubts whether it was actually Booth who died on farmer Garrett's property.

There is even an aura of mystery about the death of Stanton in December 1869. According to newspaperman Ben Perley Poore, the former War Secretary may have taken his own life. "There are many at Washington," he wrote, "who believe that Mr. Stanton committed suicide by cutting his throat with a razor."[4] The funeral was strictly private, and the attending undertaker, R. F. Harvey, steadfastly refused then or later to admit or deny anything about the cause of death.

The most intriguing postscript to the Lincoln assassination was not brought to light until 1960. At that time

Roy Neff, a New Jersey research chemist, bought a dusty bound volume of Colburn's *United Services Magazine* covering the last half of the year 1864. Some time afterward, while browsing through the book, he noticed that some of the pages had letters and numbers inscribed in pencil in the margins. It looked to him as though a code were involved, so out of curiosity he took the book to a cryptographer. An incredible two-part message, signed "Lafayette C. Baker," was found. It should be pointed out that Baker was a flamboyant man given to making statements that have been questioned by historians. Nevertheless, the enormity of his alleged message is such that it must be considered. This is especially important because chemical treatment of the pages finally revealed an actual signature of Baker's that was subsequently authenticated by handwriting experts.

The message categorically accused Stanton of being the man behind the assassination plot, and stated that Baker learned this when he approached his chief on April 10, 1865 to report the existence of the plot as he had uncovered it. "Ecert [Major Thomas L. Eckert]," it read, "had made all the contacts, the deed to be done on the fourteenth, I did not know the identity of the assassin, but I knew most all else when I approached E.S. about it." The message went on to declare that the next day Stanton, in order to blackmail Baker into silence, showed the latter a forged document which implicated him in the earlier kidnap plot. The next-to-last paragraph of the message was most startling. It said:

> There were at least eleven members of Congress involved in the plot, no less than twelve Army officers, three Naval officers and at least twenty-four civilians, of which one was a governor of a loyal state. Five were bankers of great repute, three were

nationally known newspapermen, and eleven were industrialists of great repute and wealth. There were probably more that I know nothing of.

This would indicate that there were even more than the thirty-five mentioned by Booth to Herold. The last paragraph of the message stated that all the conspirators were named in the bound volume of the same magazine covering the first half of 1864. It also claimed that these men had contributed $85,000 toward the assassination. The concluding lines were, "Only eight persons know the details of the plot and the identity of the others. I fear for my life. L.C.B."

Lafayette C. Baker died at the age of forty-four on July 3, 1868. It was reported in the press that he died of typhoid fever. His death certificate gave meningitis as the cause of death. Journalist-historian John Cottrell has asserted that Baker was poisoned.[5] To borrow a phrase from Winston Churchill, the deeper one gets into the Lincoln assassination, the more it appears to be "a riddle wrapped in a mystery inside an enigma." Many are bound to question the validity of this 1960 revelation. It may well be authentic, but there is no way of absolutely verifying it. The first volume, supposedly containing the names of the conspirators, has not, to anyone's knowledge, turned up. Even if it does, the most it can do is add to the already ponderous collection of paper supporting this particular conspiracy theory.

Assuming the Baker message to be true, we are forced to face a new question: How could a fanatical Confederate sympathizer like John Wilkes Booth devote himself to a conspiracy headed by a man like Stanton? An avowed enemy of the South, Stanton represented everything that Booth detested. We would have to presume, then, that

Booth acted on the assumption he was working in concert with other supporters of the Confederacy. The Baker message was very clear about the fact that only eight persons knew the identities of all the conspirators. Could there be any connection here with the enigmatic line in Booth's diary which read, "I have almost a mind to return to Washington and clear my name, which I feel I can do." If Booth did have contacts whose identities have never been revealed, it is quite possible to conclude that he never knew their actual goals, and was their cat's-paw rather than their leader. But all of these conclusions must remain in the dim realm of conjecture, for the players in this tragic mystery-drama are long dead. Nevertheless, the shadows of their performance can never fade from history.

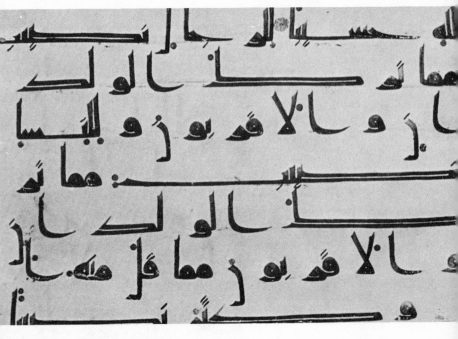

Page of the Koran, 10th century

2 Mohammed

3 Religious sacrifice

4 Mencius

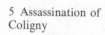

5 Assassination of Coligny

6 The death of Caesar

Catherine de Medici

8 Massacre on St. Bartholomew's Day

9 Thomas à Becket

10 Assassination of Henry IV of Navarre

11 Assassination of Henry III

12 Charles IX of France

13 Philip II, King of Macedon

14 Alexander the Great

15 Ivan the Terrible

16 Catherine the Great

17 Paul I

18 Tiberius Gracchus

19 The Nihilists published clandestine newspapers. This scene, shown in a French illustrated weekly of 1881, depicts a police raid on a Nihilist press in Kharkov.

20 Peter III of Russia

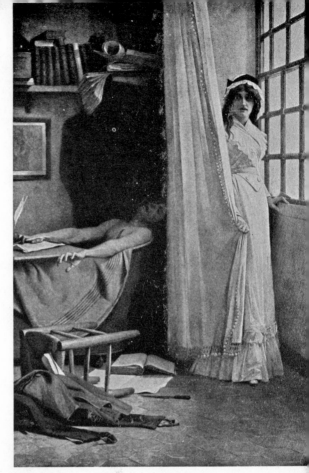

21 Charlotte Corday, with
the slain Jean Paul Marat

22 Assassination of Alexander II of Russia on March 1, 1881

23 *Left:* Gavrilo Princip, assassin of Archduke Franz Ferdinand

24 *Right:* Archduke Franz Ferdinand and his wife, Sophie, with their children, Ernst, Sophie, and Max

25 Lenin

26 *From left to right:* Adolf Hitler, Hermann Goering, and Joseph Goebbels

27 Stadium at Nuremberg packed solidly with Storm Troopers, men carrying swastika banners, and more than 100,000 persons assembled to hear Hitler's speech at the tenth Nazi Party Congress.

28 Ernst Roehm

29 Portrait of
Daniel McNaughton

30 Trial of Daniel McNaughton at London's Central Criminal Court, Old Bailey

31 Henry Thomas, Lord Cockburn, who, before his elevation to the peerage, was defense attorney for Daniel McNaughton.

34 John H. Surratt, Jr.

35 Mary Surratt

36 Lewis Paine (Powell)

37 David E. Herold

32 John Wilkes Booth

33 John Wilkes Booth in the act of shooting President Lincoln in his box at Ford's Theater.

38 Samuel Arnold

39 Michael O'Laughlin

40 Edward Spangler

41 George A. Atzerodt

42 Dr. Samuel Mudd

43 The trial of the Lincoln assassins

44 The board that tried the Lincoln assassins

45 Execution of assassins

46 Secretary of War,
Edwin M. Stanton

47 Lafayette C. Baker, after he
became a brigadier general

48 Louis (Lepke) Buchalter, in
a picture released by the F.B.I.

49 Dutch Schultz, waiting for the verdict in the
government's income tax case against him.

50 Albert Anastasia

51 Thomas E. Dewey, presenting his credentials to Governor Herbert Lehman.

52 Martin (Buggsy) Goldstein at left, with Harry (Pittsburgh Phil) Strauss, on the train on their way to Sing Sing.

53 & 54 Arnold Schuster, who led to the arrest of Willie Sutton, was found shot to death in Brooklyn.

55 Willie Sutton studiously examines his fingernails as Thomas Kling is led away, manacled to a prison guard. Both Sutton and Kling went to Sing Sing.

56 David Frankfurter in Chur, Switzerland, Courthouse, before being sentenced.

57 Wilhelm Gustloff

58 James Earl Ray being escorted from Tennessee State Prison to be taken to Memphis for his hearing.

59 Sirhan Sirhan being taken from Ambassador Hotel, Los Angeles, immediately after the shooting of Robert F. Kennedy.

60 Sirhan being interviewed by an NBC News correspondent the day after he was formally sentenced to death.

61 The dramatic moment at the Dallas City jail when Jack Ruby stepped forward and leveled a revolver at Lee Harvey Oswald. (Picture taken by Jack Beers, staff photographer of the *Dallas Morning News* and Copyright 1963 by *The Dallas Morning News*.)

62 Photograph taken at New York City's Grand Central Station as spectators watch a large-screen television presentation of President John F. Kennedy's funeral. (Associated Press Photo from New York.)

63 Alexander Hamilton—Aaron Burr duel

64 Sherman's march through Georgia

65 A group of Hatfield-McCoy feudists

7

THE
HIRED ASSASSIN

Assassins come in all sizes, shapes, colors, and ages. Yet, it would not be misleading to say that over the ages most of them have been males under thirty years of age. As the evidence has clearly indicated, the majority have been motivated by a variety of factors ranging from mental aberration and religious fanaticism to political idealism. The hired assassin stands distinctly apart from the others and, in a sense, he is the most sinister one of the lot.

He is the man who kills, not in a fit of passion, not to advance a cause, and not even out of any particular lust for killing. To be sure, some professional killers have been known to enjoy their work and to take pride in it. But this should not come as a surprise. Few men are forced to become killers against their will. The hired assassin is a journeyman killer who has much the same attitude toward tracking down his prey as the professional big-game hunter. Like that hunter, when he pulls the trigger (or employs some other lethal device) he is principally concerned with hitting the target. The fact that a life is being destroyed is immaterial. What counts is striking the fatal blow with a maximum of efficiency.

Assassins for hire have always enjoyed more status in the United States than anywhere else in the world, especially during the last century or so. Other countries have had their share of professional killers, but Americans have traditionally glorified the role of the assassin and elevated him to the position of a <u>folk hero</u>. Thus, though he has never deserved the resultant adulation, he has rarely failed to revel in it and take full advantage of it whenever possible. Although this has frequently led to the eventual downfall of many an individual killer, it has also helped to perpetuate the folk-hero image and to foster a continuing distortion of values.

Our national tradition of violence, which we will examine in the last chapter, is very much a part of this whole complex fabric. Here we will consider only one aspect of it, an aspect that has all too often been distorted by literature and the media of entertainment and news.

The individual who kills for a price is less dangerous to society at large than the habitual drunken driver, the drug addict, or the dedicated revolutionary. The drunken driver kills any innocent person unfortunate enough to cross his path at the wrong time (in 1967 alone there were approximately four motor-vehicle deaths in the United States for every homicide). The drug addict kills out of desperation, if confronted with a choice between killing to get what he craves and doing without it. The revolutionary is dedicated to the destruction of established society, and he believes that the end justifies the means. If a few innocent lives must be snuffed out in the course of achieving that end, he thinks nothing of snuffing them out. The man who kills for a price regards indiscriminate killing as foolish and unprofitable. He is as likely to kill anyone without getting paid for it as a banker is to lend money at no interest.

Rarely is a professional killer unstable. He cannot afford to be, nor can his employers. In his book, *The Hired Killers,* author Peter Wyden wrote:

> Generally these murderers are neither irrational nor unintelligent. Their backgrounds are decidedly troubled, but not more so than the past histories of our fellow citizens. Friends, employers, and penal authorities often considered them fair risks for adjustment.[1]

Wyden was referring specifically to a group of professional and semi-professional killers about whom he wrote in depth in his book. But what he had to say about them was reasonably applicable to most others.

The most alarming fact about professional killers is that the most successful of them are never caught; they are never thrust into the harsh glare of publicity, and are rarely, if ever, even suspected. They go about their business unobtrusively, indistinguishable from their fellow citizens, and frequently maintaining strong family and community ties. But these are the real professionals, not the part-timers who occasionally commit a murder in amateur fashion for amateur conspirators, and the overwhelming majority of them are employed in the ranks of organized crime.

Crime and criminals are social phenomena, and though the costs of organized crime are staggering, and affect everyone in society, they do not appear as factors in the monthly cost-of-living index. Yet, when large shipments of expensive commodities such as liquor, applicances, and cigarettes are hijacked, insurance companies pay for the losses and premium rates go up for everyone. When racket-oriented labor unions force businesses to pay extortion, kickbacks, and spurious welfare funds, the cost is passed on to the public in the form of higher prices. There is so much money involved annually that crime is big business, and in terms of capital was once compared by underworld leader Meyer Lansky to General Motors.

When a union leader is murdered as a result of a criminal conspiracy, it is an assassination. When a business executive is slain for reasons related to his occupation it is an assassination. When anyone is deliberately killed under conditions other than those categorized as a crime of passion, it is an assassination. Most of the sensational gangland murders are assassinations, and many are political. A perfect case in point is the slaying of the Prohibition mobster, Dutch Schultz. During the course of his unsavory career, the Dutchman, as he was often called, was involved in the sale of illegal beer, the numbers racket, labor-union racketeering, slot machines, and other assorted gambling enterprises.

In order to remain in business without being molested by the authorities, Dutch Schultz spent large sums of money for bribes and to ensure the elections of crooked politicians who would protect him once they were in office. A vicious man who thought nothing of killing anyone he suspected was cheating him, he was hated and feared for good reason. Even fellow underworld characters regarded him with distaste. By the year 1935, Prohibition was history and the men who had profited so handsomely by it were now forced to find other means of doing business. It was at this time, therefore, that they began to adopt the methods that would lead to organized crime as it came to be known a decade later. In short, they were becoming somewhat more conservative—not a great deal, but enough to indicate a few minor changes.

The situation as it existed at the end of Prohibition was accurately summed up by reporter Sid Feder, in his introduction to the book *Murder, Inc.,* written in collaboration with former Brooklyn Prosecutor Burton B. Turkus.

> The murder of one beer baron by another had come to be accepted as the elimination of unneeded surplus, but it was obvious to the gangsters that the public would hardly stand for such promiscuous slaughter once Prohibition was gone. To solve these problems, the Syndicate was born. The chief reason for its quick universal acceptance was that the end of Prohibition's crazy era brought an end to the insane egotistical ganglord of the Dutch Schultz breed who settled everything with a bullet.

The new underworld leaders were not unlike their counterparts in the world of legitimate business; hence the use of the term Syndicate. Agreement was reached among them as to which mob would control which enterprises, and in what designated territories throughout the nation. A board of directors established matters of national policy, a hierarchy was defined, and in general, the organization provided all the functions of government for those over whom it claimed jurisdiction, and who paid it allegiance. No one leader could be regarded as *the* top man. Every man on the board of directors had (and still has) the power of life and death over violators of the rules. As things worked out it was the Brooklyn branch of the Syndicate that served as the department of extermination, or, as it came to be known to the general public, Murder, Incorporated.

Essentially the men who ran Murder, Inc. were engaged in the same illegal activities as their underworld colleagues everywhere else in the country. Albert Anastasia was, until his own sensational gangland execution, undisputed boss of the Brooklyn waterfront, and Lepke Buchalter was the highest ranking underworld figure ever to die in the electric chair. In Turkus's words he was "the most powerful of all labor and industrial rackets czars." Other notables included Mendy Weiss, who died with Lepke at Sing Sing; Abe "Kid Twist" Reles, trigger man turned state's witness, who jumped, fell, or was pushed to his death from a window before he could testify against his former associates; and killer Harry "Pittsburgh Phil" Strauss, known equally for his dandified dressing habits and for his enthusiasm for murder.

In 1935, young Thomas E. Dewey, an aggressive prosecutor who had made his reputation in the New York District Attorney's office, was appointed Special Prosecutor of Organized Crime by Governor Herbert Lehman. The newly formed Syndicate feared that Dewey's investigations might eventually smoke out its leaders and do the organization irreparable harm. Consequently the directors met to determine what should be done about this growing threat.

Although Dutch Schultz operated out of Newark, New Jersey, and risked immediate arrest by New York police if he were ever caught east of the Hudson River, he threw caution to the winds and attended this all-important meeting. Dewey had caused the Dutchman any number of headaches and the Jersey ganglord was so infuriated he was willing to risk his neck to get back at the Manhattan prosecutor. In the course of the discussion it was suggested that Dewey be eliminated. Schultz made no effort to conceal his desire to have Dewey killed. Others, however, were more cautious. Although they recognized that

Dewey was a definite threat to their operations, they wanted first to determine the feasibility of a successful assassination plot. After all, they were professionals and if they were going to do the job it had to be done efficiently.

The job of making this determination was assigned to Albert Anastasia. No detail was overlooked. For four straight mornings Dewey's comings and goings were meticulously observed. It was duly noted that he customarily left his apartment with two bodyguards, went to a certain drugstore to make a telephone call to his office, then left and headed downtown.

On being assured that Dewey was "a sitting duck," further preparations were made. A car was stolen and hidden away as the getaway car for the day of the assassination. License plates were stolen from another car and transferred to the escape vehicle; guns were stolen, the serial numbers obliterated, and silencers fitted to the barrels. The plan was that the trigger man would get to the drugstore before Dewey, take his time over his purchases, and then, when Dewey arrived, would shoot him and the druggist. With silencers, no sound would be heard outside, and the gunman would have ample opportunity to slip out, get into the waiting getaway car, and vanish.

There was only one hitch to the plot. Was it really worth the inevitable uproar that would follow in the wake of Dewey's assassination? "Yes!" insisted Dutch Schultz. "Not necessarily," theorized other, cooler heads. After all, they pointed out, Dewey's jurisdiction was limited to New York's Southern District; in other words, Manhattan. If the Syndicate closed down its Manhattan operations a slight drop in revenues would result, but the overall nationwide effect would be negligible. On the other hand, if they went so far as to assassinate a prosecutor of Dewey's stature—or any prosecutor, for that matter—there would be a nationwide crackdown on organized crime that might prove disastrous to all concerned.

Why wreck the entire Syndicate just to ensure the smooth operation of activities in only one small area? That was poor business judgment. A vote was taken and it was agreed to abandon the plot to assassinate Thomas E. Dewey.

To Dutch Schultz this was a severe blow. He was concerned strictly with his own bailiwick. Furthermore, he was too unimaginative to visualize the long-range effects of such a political murder should it be carried out. He is reported to have angrily disagreed with the decision of the directors, and to have loudly volunteered, "I still say he ought to be hit, and if nobody else is gonna do it, I'm gonna hit him myself!" But of even greater significance was his reckless threat to carry out his promise within forty-eight hours. When word of this trickled back via the grapevine to the Syndicate's top echelons, a short meeting was held, and the Dutchman was sentenced to death. No one was permitted to openly defy their edicts and live, especially when the result of such defiance could jeopardize everyone concerned.

Accordingly, on the night of October 23, 1935, two high-ranking trigger men, Charlie "The Bug" Workman and Mendy Weiss (operations manager of Murder, Inc.), headed for the Palace Chophouse in Newark, New Jersey, Dutch Schultz's base of operations. In a black sedan driven by a hoodlum later identified only as "Piggy," the pair arrived at their destination shortly after ten o'clock. After checking the place over with a practiced eye, while Mendy covered the door, the Bug entered the men's room, where he spotted a slightly familiar figure bent over a wash-

basin. Assuming he was one of the Dutchman's bodyguards, Workman fired a single shot from his .45 and cautiously emerged, gun in hand, as his victim slumped to
the floor. Next, the Bug approached a table at the rear of
the barroom which was occupied by three of Schultz's
key lieutenants, Lulu Rosenkrantz, bodyguard and chauf-
feur; Ab "Misfit" Landau, trigger man; and Abbadaba
Berman, accountant. Before the trio were an adding
machine and a pile of papers, which they quickly abandoned as they reached for their pistols and opened fire on
the Bug. When the smoke had cleared away, Dutch
Schultz lay mortally wounded and his three henchmen
were dead. Actually the Dutchman had been the first to
fall, for it was he who had been washing his hands when
the fatal slug tore into his body.

The death of Dutch Schultz in a way marked the end
of an era. It had begun with the bloody gang wars that
erupted during Prohibition, when the words "criminal"
and "politician" were all too often synonymous, and disputes were settled by bullets more often than by ballots.
It ended an era when rival gangs and racketeers declared
open season on one another, and thought nothing of cutting an enemy down in a hail of machine-gun fire one
day, then sending a thousand dollars worth of flowers to
his funeral the next. Indeed, Prohibition gangleader Dion
O'Banion, whose front was a flower shop of his own,
died there, ironically, while preparing a wreath for a rival
gangster's lavish funeral. It ended a wild and lawless time
during which illegal fortunes were made overnight by
hypocritical opportunists. It ended an era forced on
America by shortsighted lawmakers who, in attempting to
legislate one aspect of public morality (in this instance,
prohibiting the consumption of alcohol), spawned a powerful underworld government which will probably never be

wholly eliminated from society unless, of course, we abandon our traditional constitutional freedoms and degenerate into a police state.

The men who did the actual job of killing on assignment were feared and respected in the underworld for their ruthlessness and professionalism. The secret of the success they enjoyed for so many years was the precision with which they approached their undertakings. First of all, they almost never killed for frivolous or personal reasons, knowing full well that if they did, they could expect neither backing nor sympathy from their bosses. Murder was treated as a precision operation that had to be carried out cleanly and efficiently. In other words, each contract, as such assassinations are still called in the underworld, had to be fulfilled with a minimum of risk.

Pittsburgh Phil once traveled from New York to Jacksonville, Florida to eliminate a victim who had been marked for death. For an entire day he trailed the man, waiting for a suitable opportunity to do the job smoothly. Finally, in a darkened movie theater he determined that the most practical way was to take a fire axe from the wall and plunge it into his quarry's skull. In the ensuing confusion he felt sure he would be able to run from the theater with the other patrons and disappear. But just as he was about to make his move his intended victim unexpectedly changed seats in order to obtain a better view of the screen. Phil was so unnerved by this he jumped up, stalked out of the theater, and took the next plane back to New York. On arrival, he explained to his superiors that he was not going to attempt a kill under any but ideal conditions. It was quite a risk he took because, according to the rules, he could have been made to pay for this failure with his own life. But by explaining immediately why he did what he did, he was not only excused, but congratulated for having chosen the correct course of action under the circumstances.

There was never any set rule as to what weapons should be employed, or how an individual killer was to go about "hitting" his target. (In the underworld, the euphemism "hit" is still used for the word "kill.") Each man was regarded as sufficiently professional to determine his own methods according to his own needs. Once a victim was marked for extermination his habits were carefully studied until the individual or team assigned to hit him were reasonably certain that they could strike and disappear without a trace. This, incidentally, was one of the chief reasons for the importation of professionals to perform underworld assassinations. A man from Brooklyn stood far less chance of being recognized in Denver or Minneapolis, and a man from San Francisco was equally unknown in Manhattan. Turkus referred to this aspect of the operation by comparing it to ordinary business.

> If a travelling salesman lives in New York and has a sales territory in Iowa, Kansas, and Nebraska, his business would hardly be classed as a New York operation. In just the same way the Brooklyn triggermen were the travelling salesmen of the national crime cartel.[3]

Another important aspect of the Murder, Inc. operation was that their gunmen were not for hire in the same sense that an automobile or apartment may be rented by anyone willing to pay the price. Assassination was used by the Syndicate only to eliminate anyone who interfered with its business, posed a threat to it anywhere, violated the rules, or failed miserably in an important assignment. Under these circumstances, assassination or the threat of death serves as a greater deterrent against transgression than capital punishment has ever been. The reason for this is clear, simple, and widely understood. There are no constitutional guarantees or legal protections operating in the underworld. The system is pure despotism in the oldest sense, and one of its most potent weapons is fear. A death sentence is a death sentence. There are only judges and executioners; there are no appeals and rarely any reprieves.

For the most part, Murder, Inc. restricted its slayings to members of its own subculture and kept hands off outsiders as long as those outsiders minded their own business. But it never hesitated to deal ruthlessly with anyone if it was convinced that its own interests would be served in the process.

A perfect example is the Arnold Schuster case. Until his capture on the night of February 18, 1952, bank robber Willie "the actor" Sutton was one of the F.B.I.'s ten most-wanted criminals in America. Authorities had urged the public to cooperate with the police, and notify them if Sutton were seen anywhere, for it was strongly believed that the elusive holdup man was somewhere in the New York area. These suspicions were verified when Schuster, a 24-year-old clothing store salesman, spotted Sutton buying an auto battery at a service station and notified police. In the flood of publicity following Willie Sutton's capture, Schuster was hailed as a public-spirited citizen. But his triumph ended abruptly in a fusillade of bullets at about 9:15 P.M. on March 8, 1952. Although the murder weapon was traced to a stolen arms shipment, the trigger man was never caught.

According to a veteran New York crime reporter who covered the story, it was generally believed by police and newspaper men that Albert Anastasia, after having seen Schuster on television, "went into a rage, because he was a little bit in his cups, and put out the word to hit the kid." Chances are slim that the killer will ever be caught.

Police believe that the one suspect in the case is dead. This is why the average citizen today does not want to get involved. He knows that the authorities will not or cannot protect him, and he has no intention of ending his life violently and prematurely as Arnold Schuster did. His death served as a sharp warning to the public and constituted a notable victory for the underworld.

Despite the rules and regulations, individual gunmen have not been averse to attempting some occasional freelance work. In certain circles of American society it is not a difficult matter to arrange "accidents" for a price. A broken arm, a shattered nose, or a few caved-in ribs can be arranged for relatively cheaply. The price of a human life is somewhat higher. No one talks about this often, and when they do it is in a highly guarded manner. But underworld bosses recognize the fact that apprentice assassins must get their training somewhere. If they can earn money during that apprenticeship, so much the better. Thus, they are hired out on a limited basis for less important contracts. Perhaps a wealthy businessman with connections wishes to arrange the permanent removal of a partner, a wife, or a troublesome girl friend. All he has to do is place a discreet phone call to a certain person, who in turn relays the information to other persons. A price is arranged, money changes hands—cash, of course— and eventually the designated victim meets with an accident, disappears, or is slain "in sensational gangland fashion" for no apparent reason. Thus young hoods are transformed into seasoned killers and innocent persons into corpses.

It is on the highest levels that the important contracts are handled. Here, when a mob-dominated union decides to move into an unorganized business, or when the mob first takes over the union, a straightforward approach is made first. If the parties who have been initially contacted are sufficiently intimidated at the outset, there is no violence, and the takeover is accomplished. If the representatives of the Syndicate meet with resistance, pressures are applied: perhaps someone is beaten, or a small fire breaks out, or a minor bombing occurs. If these pressure tactics don't work, stronger measures are employed, and finally men die. It is the knowledge on the part of the victims that lives will most assuredly be lost if they do not give in to extortion that enables the perpetrators of organized crime to succeed. Also present is the unfortunate lack of faith in police ability to afford adequate protection. Most significant, however, is the deep penetration of the underworld into politics and so-called legitimate business.

Murder, Inc. is long since out of business as a thriving Brooklyn enterprise. Seven of its key men died in the electric chair in 1941. But organized crime and professional killers still exist. The picture has changed radically since the 1940's: headline-making murders of men like Bugsy Siegel and Albert Anastasia occur much less often. The directors of the underworld monopoly are growing more concerned with their stock dividends and Swiss bank accounts. They are far more secure in their position today, and they do not resort to assassinations as often as they once did. In the age of electronics, computers, and jets, communications are better, profits are more substantial, and murder is not as essential a business practice as it once was. But it has never been completely abandoned as an effective means of dealing with difficult problems, and it will probably continue to be used as long as even the slightest possibility of a demand for it remains.

8

Wednesday
Thurs.
Tues,
Wed.
Thurs.

ASSASSINATION and TERRORISM: CAUSE and EFFECT

Certainly one of the most basic questions concerning the subject of assassinations is, "What causes them?" That there are any number of excuses to justify assassination and its companion, terrorism, is increasingly apparent. But excuses and eloquent rationales can obscure the truth more often than not. In *Assassination and Political Violence* Professor Carl Leiden has said, "A sufficient requirement for assassination is the existence of one man appropriately motivated. Any society spawns a portion of such individuals; chance, circumstance, opportunity, and so on will account for the presence or lack of isolated assassinations of this kind."[1]

An outstanding example of assassination in this context occurred in the resort town of Davos, Switzerland, on February 4, 1936. The victim was Wilhelm Gustloff, a German national, and acknowledged number one Nazi in that country. The assassin was 27-year-old David Frankfurter, a Jewish medical student of Yugoslavian citizenship, who stated his impressions and motives quite clearly when

interviewed later. Having purchased an automatic pistol
well in advance of the deed, he weighed the matter in
his mind for some time. Then, when he had resolved to
go ahead with it, he went directly to Gustloff's house,
rang the doorbell, was admitted by his intended victim's
wife, and waited patiently for his opportunity to strike.
He is quoted by Emil Ludwig, in *The Davos Murder*, as
having said:

> While waiting, I had in front of me a life-size portrait of Hitler
> . . . it was a symbolic shot I fired. . . . In my homeland the path
> of serious endeavor is barred against Jews. Not everyone is able
> to submit tamely. In Switzerland when anyone is given a clout on
> the side of the head, he is likely to return the blow with interest.
> . . . I had no personal grievance. My family has not suffered. I am
> a Jew. I was impelled by idealistic motives. . . . I have grown ex-
> tremely fond of Switzerland. It seemed to me disgusting that such
> a cur should soil the good things here. . . . Gustloff wanted to
> make a vassal state out of Switzerland. . . . I am a medical student,
> and he gave me the impression that he was a bacillus through
> whom a virulent pestilence might be introduced into Switzerland.
> It was the pestilence I aimed at, not the person.[2]

Frankfurter had visited relatives in Germany on several
occasions, and was highly motivated by what he saw happening there, especially as a member of the group that
was the principal target of Nazi oppression. After a trial
before five judges in a court at Chur, Switzerland, he was
convicted on December 14, 1936, and given the maximum
sentence of eighteen years imprisonment.

Before probing more deeply into the root causes of
assassination it would be useful first to examine the various
categories into which it falls. Up to now we have dealt
mostly with specific assassins and assassination events,
and others will be discussed later. But now it is appro-

priate to categorize assassination in order to understand more about causes and effects. In Volume 8 of the Staff Report to the National Commission on the Causes and Prevention of Violence, the authors neatly spelled out such categories in terms of social and political context and reasons, saying:

1. The first category we can identify is assassination by one political elite to replace another without effecting any substantial systemic or ideological change. The purpose of such an assassination is simply to change the identity of the top man and the ruling clique . . .

   This type of assassination has been successful in countries where the government has little de facto impact on the vast body of citizens outside the capital city. As long as governments can come and go with little impact or participation by peons or *fellahin,* as the case may be, palace revolutions appear to be a practical way of gaining power. This type of assassination has not appeared in the United States.

2. A second category is assassination for the purpose of terrorizing and destroying the legitimacy of the ruling elite in order to effect substantial systemic or ideological change.

   Such assassination may be directed against high government officials or against mid-level officials to determine the effectiveness of the central government at the local or provincial level. When such terror is directed at a chief of state, the assassin may accomplish his goal even though the attempt is unsuccessful . . .

This point was emphatically stated by author John Williams who wrote in his book, *Heyday for Assassins,* "Part of the attraction of this drastic form of terrorism for the revolutionaries, extremists and eccentrics was no doubt its spectacular nature, for assassination—like justice—must not only be done, it must be seen to be done." Elaborating further on this category of assassination, the commission staff report continues:

Our studies show that this kind of assassination is effective in achieving the long-range goals sought, although not in advancing the short-term goals or careers of the terrorists themselves. Our studies show that, at least in modern history (post 1850), it cannot be said that in the long run any terrorist group was unsuccessful, except in those countries such as Soviet Russia and Nazi Germany where the ruling elite was willing to use massive counterterror to suppress potentially terroristic groups. Once a terrorist group is well established, the only effective response is either counterterror or agreement to the basic demands of the terrorists—demands which may or may not be compatible with a democratic society . . .

We cannot overemphasize the alarming nature of these conclusions—that terrorism has always succeeded in effectuating its long-range goals *except* when dealt with by counterterror. To feel secure in the knowledge that terror can be dealt with when the government has broad popular support, and is able to control terror without resorting to counterterror is one thing, but suppose right-wing extremists managed to get control of the United States government in reaction to left-wing terrorist activities. If that were to happen, it is not illogical to predict that strict measures of counterterror would be applied to the leftists, and eventually to all who opposed the rightists in power. On the other hand, if the leftists were to succeed in their terrorism and eventually seize control of the country, they, too, would unhesitatingly deal with opposition by means of more terrorism. Professor Feliks Gross summed it up concisely when he wrote:

Violence has generated violence; blood has called, in the past for more blood. Terror, even in the name of the highest ideals, has created, in the end, political habits that have moved into the patterns of political life, and have continued even after conditions were changed.[6]

This is not exaggeration. In the 1930's the United States government narrowly escaped overthrow by a military *coup d'état* at the hands of a rightist, high-ranking military group. When President Roosevelt learned about it, he took immediate and effective steps. The leader of the would-be *coup* was sent to a post far enough away to prevent further mischief on his part, and without his leadership the plot fizzled. The danger continues to exist. No less an authority on such matters than William L. Shirer, author of *The Rise and Fall of the Third Reich,* has declared that of all the non-totalitarian nations today, the United States is the most likely to go fascist via the democratic process. If this were the assertion of some left-wing radical Cassandra, it could be taken lightly, but it is the warning of a respected journalist-historian who recognizes the danger signs when he sees them.

The implications here are grim indeed. It is not difficult to envision what could happen in America in the event of a massive, organized campaign of terrorism. Faced with a choice between the alternatives of repression and concession (to terror), the Establishment would undoubtedly choose repression. It would not be a repression quite like that of Nazi Germany or the Communist bloc police states; it would be sugarcoated, subtle, and palatable to the "silent majority" who do not fear extremism when applied to the defense of their own moral values. Most fundamental is the fact that those who wield power in the United States have the weapons and the technology to maintain it.

The lessons taught by history on the subject of terror are very clear. It succeeded in Southern Ireland against the British. The British also tried to fight it in Cyprus

and failed, and they were hardly any more successful
against it in India, in Palestine, and Egypt, to mention
only a few examples. The French succumbed in Algeria,
and to a certain extent in Indochina, but with a difference
there. To revolutionaries, each act of terror is an act of
war. A government official who dies at the hands of an
assassin may be regarded by his compatriots as a murder
victim, but to those who kill him he is nothing more than
a casualty of war.

There are domestic lessons, too, that are very much a
part of the American heritage. The assassination of Abraham Lincoln caused a great deal of short-lived rejoicing
in the ranks of unreconstructed rebels, who did not antic-
ipate the extent to which some Northerners would over-
react. They found out soon enough when harsh, repressive
measures were taken by former enemies bent on forcing
them back into the Union, finishing by political means
the defeat that had been inflicted militarily. Some
Northerners came to the South to work for Reconstruction
with a genuine spirit of reconciliation. Many, however,
sought to punish and avenge, while unscrupulous opportunists among them openly determined to get what they
could while they could. To the Southerners, stinging
under the humiliation of defeat, they were all "damyankee
carpetbaggers."

In short the Northerners among them came to be regarded by the southern populace as illegitimate oppressors;
in other words, a foreign elite, a troublesome occupying
force. Indeed, to this day residents of some southern districts refer to strangers as "furriners." In any event a
wave of terrorism and assassination broke out. It became
common practice for Southerners to assassinate Northerners holding southern political offices, and to conduct

deliberate campaigns against Southerners, especially blacks, who collaborated with them.

Although some of the terrorists were southern opportunists taking advantage of anti-Yankee feelings to further their own ends, or to commit out-and-out crimes, many were simply incapable of loving their former enemies. The depth of their hatred is unequivocally stated in the following excerpt of a letter from a Mississippi woman to her Confederate soldier husband, following the destruction of the town of Brandon, Miss. by federal troops:

> The thieving rascals reached our premises whilst we were at the dinner table on Sunday, and kept up their plundering and stealing until dark. Every horse and mule Papa had was taken away, hogs killed, and all the poultry taken. In the smoke house nothing was left, except some meal which they emptied on the floor . . .
>
> In the house there was not a trunk, drawer, wardrobe, desk or anything they did not plunder and plunder well; and the contents scattered over the house, and everything stolen they wished. Not a garment of yours did they leave . . . what was left was torn to pieces or abused in some way. Papa has nothing left but what he was wearing. Every bed was stripped of clothing. For three meals we hadn't a thing but roasted potatoes to eat, and since that time what we have eaten has been done with our fingers; not a knife, or a fork was left, and but little earthenware. . . .
>
> All this stealing was done before our eyes and neither words nor tears could prevent it. I hate them more now than I did the evening I saw them sneaking off with all we cared for, and so it will be every day I live.[7]

The Ku Klux Klan was an outgrowth of post-Civil War terrorism, and the overall campaign was so successful that the South effectively reestablished the old antebellum way of life, which was not forced to face any serious challenges from outside until well into the 1950's.

The immediate result of such relatively recent chal-

lenges as civil rights legislation, and what many southerners regard as a twentieth-century Yankee invasion has
been a cultural clash of such severe proportions that it
may require another century or more before northern and
southern Americans can permanently resolve their differences. The rekindling of old bitterness and hatreds has
only generated more violence, more terror, and more
assassination. Certainly every violent death in the course
of the civil rights movement in America falls into the
category of assassination aimed at terror and the destruction of the legitimacy of the ruling elite. But as civil
rights activists become more fragmented among themselves, as blacks and whites become more polarized, as
right- and left-wing extremists become more radical, and
agitate for more violence, and as rhetoric gives way to
rioting, sniping, and bombing, victims of assassination
will increase.

There is an alternative, however, which offers a note of
optimism on the basis of past history. The staff report to
the commission phrases it succinctly as follows:

> The best defense against terrorism is a government which has
> the broad popular support to control terrorist activities through
> normal channels of law enforcement without resorting to counter-
> terror. Terrorists often correctly perceive that their greatest enemy
> is the moderate who attempts to remedy whatever perceived injus-
> tices form the basis for terrorist strength. It is often these mod-
> erates who are targets of assassination.[8]

Thus, assassination as an act of terrorism must be considered as separate and distinct from assassination arising
out of any other motive. It is a political act, strictly calculated as a step toward attaining a specific goal. In committing such an assassination, the perpetrators know perfectly well that the victim, were he permitted to live, might

well attain the same goals to which they give lip service, and thereby gain political advantage for himself and political allies. In other words, the terrorists, despite the high-sounding quality of the ideals they claim to have, are more concerned with seizing power than they are with working for the public good regardless of where the power rests.

Therefore, it is every individual's responsibility to question not just the ideals and goals of the potential terrorist, but the true nature of his concern for the public welfare. If the public welfare is his primary concern, then he is willing to concede that there may be more than one way of achieving it. If power is his principal objective, then he will insist, often in the most emphatic of terms, that his way is the only way.

The third category of assassination as defined by the authors of the commission's staff report is "assassination by the government in power to suppress political challenge." This is the approach taken by totalitarian governments. The report continues:

> Such strategy is not necessarily ideologically based. Machiavelli advised this strategy for the prince who had just come to power— to kill relatives of the previous prince and other potential challengers with promptness in order to make his power secure. Such a strategy is an indication and confession of weakness by the central government. [It presupposes a recognition on the part of the authorities that they lack the necessary qualities to withstand any challenge.] This type of assassination has not occurred in the United States.[9]

The fourth category consists of assassination for propaganda purposes. It is what the staff report calls "the so-called 'propaganda of the deed' popular with anarchists at the turn of the century." This immediately brings to

mind the bloody centuries of turmoil that have plagued
Ireland since the Welsh-Norman conquest of the twelfth
century. As time passed in that strife-ridden country the
names of the terrorist organizations changed, but the
victims were always the same—symbols of the English
government or, as it has been called, the Anglo-Irish
Ascendancy. Whether the Irish patriots were Fenians, Land
Leaguers, members of the Sinn Fein or, later on, the I.R.A.,
they were bound by ties of fervent Irish Nationalism.
Their chief problem was a lack of cohesiveness and central leadership. While some were moderate, others were
extremist, and those who advocated violence and assassination practiced what they preached.

One such group, calling themselves the Invincibles, was
a breakaway organization of ultra-extremist Fenians. They
decided to assassinate the permanent Under Secretary of
the Irish Parliament, Thomas Henry Burke. They despised
him as a "castle rat"—the derisive Fenian term used to
describe Irish Catholics loyal to the British, and derived
from the fact that the seat of government was located at
Dublin Castle.

Although their organization lacked finesse insofar as
secrecy, efficiency, and the ability to cover their tracks
were concerned, the Invincibles succeeded, on May 6,
1882, in assassinating Burke and his companion, Lord
Frederick Cavendish, the newly installed Chief Secretary of
State, who had arrived in Dublin only that day. As the
two statesmen walked alone through the gathering dusk
in Phoenix Park a little after seven P.M. they were attacked by the waiting assassins who, after a short, violent
struggle, finished them off with surgical knives that had
been smuggled over from London for the purpose.

Although the Invincibles who had been actively involved

in the deed were eventually brought to trial and five of them hanged, they were certainly successful in creating "propaganda of the deed." That they were assassins in the classic sense, as distinguished from common murderers, was clearly pointed out by Tighe Hopkins, who wrote about the case in an English magazine article in 1896. He said:

> These men, it is to be remarked, had nothing in the nature of a private wrong to avenge. Not a man among them had ever in his lifetime suffered directly or indirectly the smallest injustice at the hands of Mr. Burke. To one and all of them he was a name and nothing more.

Although they never said so in as many words, the Irish Invincibles believed exactly what Itzhak Yizernitsky, a leader of the Jewish terrorist organization, *Lohmey Heruth Israel* (better known as the Stern Gang), wrote years later: "A man who goes forth to take the life of another he does not know must believe one thing only— that by his act he will change the course of history." Openly admitting their admiration for Irish terrorists, Jewish counterparts in Palestine carried on an unrelenting campaign against the British until the state of Israel became a fact. Certainly there could be no clearer expression of intent than the following passage from the *Lohmey Heruth Israel* journal, *Hazit.*

> Now this is the law of our war. So long as there is fear in the heart of any Jew in the world, so long as there are embers burning under our feet anywhere in the world, so long as there is a foreign policeman guarding the gates of our homeland, so long as there is a foreign master over our country, so long as we do not rule in our own land, so long shall we be in your way. You will look around you in fear day and night. You will sleep in your uniforms, you will wear your arms, your life here will be hell day and night,

150 SOCIETY AND THE ASSASSIN

for we have had our fill of shame and exile, slavery and humiliation, for we are weary of waiting, begging and praying, for we
have taken the oath—the freedom of Israel.[11]

Later, after failing in an attempt to assassinate the British High Commissioner, Sir Harold MacMichael, *Hazit*
said, "We did not single him out because he is MacMichael;
the punishment is not personal; the fire was aimed at the
High Commissioner of a foreign rule. . ." Indeed, though
MacMichael was fortunate enough to return to England
alive, his successor, Lord Moyne, was assassinated by two
young dedicated terrorists, one of whom, Eliahu Bet Zouri,
said after being captured: "Some men live short lives in
which nothing significant happens. That is a tragedy. But
to live a short life which includes a deed for one's mother-
land . . . that is a triumph . . . If it must be so, I am
happy to give my life, for I know that our nation will
benefit by the deed." And *that* (excluding the mentally
ill) is the reasoning of any idealistic assassin, be he Irish,
Jewish, Arab, or American, whether we applaud or exe-
crate his action. This is also the reason behind the most
recent manifestations of assassination for propaganda purposes, such as the deaths of foreign diplomats at the
hands of South American terrorists and the blowing up of
airline passengers by Arab extremists.

The fifth and final category of assassination as described
by the commission's staff report is the one that is unconnected with "rational political goals" and "satisfies only the
pathological needs of the mentally disturbed attacker. This
represents the typical attacker of Presidents of the United
States. Whether such assassinations achieve the goal of the
assassin is a matter of psychiatric speculation. To the
extent that such assassins seek attention, publicity, and
importance, they consistently have achieved their goals
in the United States."

Within the framework of the five stated categories of assassination there are certain other factors, variable from country to country, that affect assassination. Circumstances often arise which help to create a climate for assassination. Sometimes it may be nothing more complicated than domestic political turmoil. As Edward Hyams pointed out in his controversial book, *Killing No Murder:* ". . . between 1918 and 1922 the various Nationalist [German] parties assassinated three hundred liberal and left-wing politicians." On the other hand, as we have seen, this climate may be induced by means of externally generated turmoil. Certainly in countries governed by uninvited foreigners, where foreign laws are enforced by occupying troops, assassination and terrorism are bound to be commonplace. It makes no difference to the terrorists if harsh retaliatory measures are taken against them. They know the rules of the game and they are fully prepared to pay the consequences when they lose a round. What matters is that the enemy be kept constantly cognizant that he is unwanted.

Essentially, then, the atmosphere is ripe for assassination and terror wherever there is oppressive rule, or what is regarded by a substantial segment of the population as oppressive rule. Under such conditions three precursors to assassination are set forth by the authors of the commission staff report:

(1) the existence of a political party with an ideology and technique of direct action.
(2) perception of oppression.
(3) presence of activists, i.e., persons willing to respond with violence to the conditions of oppression.

It makes no difference in the final analysis what the activists' personal politics may be, for if they choose to

adopt terror and/or assassination as the means to their
ends, they must be labeled as extremists. As such they
often bear a closer resemblance to their bitterest enemies
at the opposite end of the pole than to moderates in their
own camp. The terrorist's existence is so precarious that
his chances of survival are poor. If he does not die violently during the course of his activities, he faces the
danger of mellowing as he grows older and turning into
a moderate himself. Part of this is related to the aging
process; the older a person becomes, the more reluctant
he is to jeopardize his life. But as long as men and women
who have reached the limits of their ability to endure
frustrations are provided with causes, movements, and
leaders who can inflame their minds and provide them
with weapons, there will be a continuous pool of terrorists.
For every individual who fails or finds a less violent
outlet for the emotions there will be a replacement. Rather
than deal with them after the fact, it is the responsibility
of society to keep the climate of violence from reaching
epidemic proportions.

9

MASS MEDIA
and ASSASSINATION

Nowadays, the relation between mass media and any social phenomenon is as complex as an infinity of mirrors. Instantaneous communication has changed the world so thoroughly that it would be a mistake to restrict our thinking to cause and effect. Certainly many responsible persons throughout the world are becoming increasingly alarmed over violence in the media. But for every attack on violence as depicted in motion pictures, on television, and on the printed page, there is a counter argument favoring it. Are people, either young or old, incited to violence by the mass media, or do they sublimate their own violent impulses by identifying with what they see or read? Still other questions arise. Are they completely unaffected? Is the depiction of violence actually a mirror of life as it actually exists and, therefore, not a cause of violence at all?

The questions are valid, but answers to them—if there are definitive answers—would not be relevant to assassination as we have been examining it so far. In order to

153

154

shed real light on the relation of mass media to assassination we must probe other areas.

One aspect that has not been touched on so far is availability of weapons. There is no relation between availability of weapons and the mass media in a society that has rigid censorship, but where freedom of speech and the press is a fact of life the relationship is unmistakable. There are relatively mild restrictions on the interstate sale of weapons, but Americans can purchase them through the mails with only a minimum of inconvenience. If it were not for the advertisements in numerous publications devoted to sports, hunting, and shooting, many owners of firearms would be hard-pressed to obtain them. This is not necessarily an attack on such publications. None of them openly advocates criminal acts, but they do contribute to the maintenance of a multi-million-dollar arms industry that is incapable of controlling weapon distribution to the extent that is necessary. Legitimate sportsmen and gun enthusiasts are, for the most part, highly responsible persons, much less likely than others to commit rash acts with firearms. But there is no way of preventing irresponsible individuals from subscribing to mass-produced publications or from obtaining weapons by illegitimate means.

The explosive combination comes into existence when extremism, weapon availability, and mass-media communications techniques are brought together (i.e. propaganda, advertising, printing, and distribution). Here are some concrete examples: In 1968, the American Nazi Party (technically, the National Socialist White People's Party) formed a subsidiary called NS Arms to handle the sale of guns through the mail. They advertised such items as 12-gauge 5-shot rapid-fire riot guns, semi-automatic rifles billed as "the perfect rapid-fire sniper rifle," armor-piercing ammunition, .25-caliber semi-automatic pistols, and Chemical Mace. The first bulletin offering these items concluded with the following statement:

> The federal government has and will do everything in its power to see that Whites are disarmed. National Socialists must arm themselves and as many other White men who can be found to fight in the coming war—while there is still time.
> HEIL HITLER[1]

In the bi-weekly tabloid, *The Black Panther,* Chairman Bobby Seale was quoted on May 18, 1968 as saying, "Every Black man should have a shotgun, a .357 magnum or a .38 in his pad to defend it . . . every woman should understand that weapon. . . ." And in the so-called "Executive Mandate #3," signed by Huey Newton, and published on March 16, 1968, the following passage appeared:

> It is . . . mandated as a general order to all members of the Black Panther Party for Self-Defense that all members must acquire the technical equipment to defend their homes and their dependents and shall do so. Any member of the Party having such technical equipment who fails to defend his threshold shall be expelled from the Party for life.[2]

In the right-wing Minuteman organization's *Bulletin,* of January 1966, this question was posed to members:

> Suppose the reader has no gun at all and is planning to buy one gun only . . . What shall it be? Though it will surprise many people my recommendation is a .22 caliber semi-automatic pistol . . .
> It's true that the .22 lacks the "shock" effect of a more powerful cartridge, but this is largely compensated for by the ease of putting a well-placed cartridge into the heart or brain. When needed for a second well-aimed shot it can be fired quicker from a .22 than from a more powerful weapon.[3]

Naturally, the above examples are the products of extremist minorities whose activities are no secret to those federal agencies charged with protecting the public. There are indications, however, of tactical shifts, on both the right and the left. In light of federal restrictions on firearms sales through the mail, certain publications favored by extremists are adopting a kind of crypto-euphemism in their mail-order sales promotion of weapons. "Antiques" and "war mementoes" are immediately recognized by insiders as firearms, ammunition, commando knives, grenades, bayonets, and (significantly) Nazi insignia and related paraphernalia.

On the extreme left, militant radicals have moved in the direction of increased violence. A member of this faction, who refused to permit the publication of his name, gave an interview to writer Gail Sheehy of *New York* Magazine (April 6, 1970) in which he discussed, among other things, the bombings of various Manhattan office buildings that housed large corporations. He said, "I'm not sure the kind of people who work in those buildings shouldn't be blown away too."

Sensational acts of violence attract the news media because they provide dramatic stories and guarantee wide coverage. Terrorist attacks on buildings, bridges, department stores, and monuments are serious, but when people get killed the situation approaches the emergency level. The irony of this is that the news media are obliged to report such events to the public; therefore, there is no way of preventing the perpetrators from obtaining the wanted publicity for their deeds.

The greatest inherent danger here is one which simply cannot be avoided. It is the possibility that psychotics or psychopaths may at any time commit acts of violence ranging anywhere from minor arson to the assassination of a public figure merely to attract attention and achieve temporary notoriety. Under totalitarian regimes, where the mass media are nothing more than official propaganda outlets, absolute censorship prevents such publicity. There are no advertisements for weapons, which in any case are not available to the general public (with the exception of places like China and Cuba, where a large civilian militia has access to state-provided arms). There is no sensational news coverage of anything disapproved by the authorities; indeed, no coverage at all of news deemed unfavorable. Under the circumstances, assassinations are rare, and if they are even attempted they are seldom reported. A notable exception apparently occurred in Moscow early in 1969, according to the following Reuters dispatch, datelined London, January 26, and carried in the New York *Times* on January 28, 1969:

> The Sunday *Times* [of London] reported today that the gunman who fired at a car occupied by four astronauts entering the Kremlin Wednesday was in the uniform of the elite Kremlin guard. The paper's Moscow correspondent, Edmund Stevens, wrote that the man emerged from a sentry box and fired five shots at the third car—not the second as earlier reported—of the procession honoring four Soviet astronauts. The correspondent said that the astronauts' car and another had changed places in the motorcade just before reaching the Moscow River Bridge leading to the Kremlin. In the below-zero weather, he added, it was virtually impossible to identify the occupants in the closed cars—all in fur caps and heavy overcoats. The gunman was thought to have been aiming for the Soviet leaders who accompanied the astronauts in the motorcade.

Swift, efficient action on the part of the Soviet police, and silence on the part of the Soviet press kept the outcome of the incident under wraps. It is a perfect illustration of what occurs in a state where the maintenance of law and

order is held to be more important than the maintenance of
free expression.

Inevitably, the traditional American freedom of speech
and expression gives rise to chaos, and indeed, sometimes
produces alarming extremism as an unpleasant side effect.
But with the leeway provided by our system, extremists are
often rendered less effective by the expression of contrary
views. There are times, however, when restraint is necessary. Certainly, if James Earl Ray and Sirhan Sirhan had
been tried under completely open, unrestricted conditions,
not only would it have been impossible for them to have
received fair trials, but it is entirely conceivable that they
themselves might have been the targets of would-be
assassins. But there are other factors involved here. When
a man like Dr. Martin Luther King is assassinated and
the killer is apprehended, the law should not permit him
to plead guilty, as Ray did. Ray's guilty plea prevented
any trial, fair or otherwise, which, if held, might possibly
have provided answers to questions the public has a right
to have answers to. As matters stand, the only man who
can answer any of these questions, James Earl Ray, cannot be forced to talk, and may never do so.

Sirhan, on the other hand, was indicted for murder in
the State of California. There a plea of guilty was impossible under the law, because the existence of the death
penalty makes such a plea tantamount to suicide. But
since it was a known fact that Sirhan had actually fired
the weapon that killed Senator Robert F. Kennedy, the
trial, though necessarily an ultra-proper one from the
standpoint of the authorities, was essentially a means of
providing information to the public. The fact that Lee
Harvey Oswald never lived to stand trial is a glaring
example of how important a trial is, for as time passes,

the doubt increases as to whether he actually killed President Kennedy.

In earlier times, American courts were sometimes more like carnivals than bars of justice. There was a general lack of decorum, and participants frequently attended trials fully armed. This often brought about outbreaks of violence, which occasionally degenerated into gunbattles and resulted in senseless fatalities. In frontier towns and open country where such violence was frequently the result of factional squabbling, irresponsible, inexperienced journalists occasionally took sides and used the press to promote the particular cause they espoused, thereby inciting further violence. Understandably, such things could take place only in a less sophisticated society than the one that has evolved during the twentieth century.

After the new century began, voices could be heard that opposed unrestrained freedom of the press. In 1916, an angry lawyer named Henry Forster addressed the Society for Medical Jurisprudence and attacked this freedom, holding up, as his example, the older, somewhat more restrictive British court regulations in respect to the press, saying:

> No trial by newspaper, no publicity bureau work is allowed while any action, whether criminal or civil, is pending; only a true and fair report of evidence and court proceedings is allowed to be published *pendente lite* [pending the suit], sweat box and third degree are unknown among the police and prosecutors. Trial by newspaper and publicity bureau work *pendente lite* are suppressed by vigorous enforcement of the common law in relation to contempt of court.[4]

In the days before instantaneous transmission of news, a sensational event such as the assassination of a world leader did not become widely known until after the passage of some time. Distances seemed greater then because travel was slower and more difficult. Assassinations in Europe did not arouse intense reactions in America and vice versa. Even today the shock value of any assassination varies according to distance and the amount of time elapsed between the event itself and general knowledge of it. The stature of the victim, of course, is the primary factor. When Gandhi was assassinated the entire world reacted with shock. Even if the victim is relatively unknown as an individual, but important because of what he represents, public reaction will be strong. The world-wide reaction to the March 1970 slaying of the West German ambassador by Guatemalan terrorists is a clear illustration of this fact. Typical of penetrating mass-media response in such a case was that of syndicated columnist Max Lerner, who wrote in the New York *Post,* April 8, 1970:

> We miss the real point about the slaying of the German ambassador in Guatemala if we think of it only as the crisis of diplomatic security. It is the moral crisis that goes deep to the breaking of the human bond. To understand it, one must focus on the glacial, dehumanized rage in the hearts of Count Karl von Spreti's assassins.

Combine the elements of wide coverage with the assassination of an international figure, and the resultant shock increases immensely. The assassination of President John F. Kennedy is the most outstanding example of this. First, the murder of a President of the United States would be shocking in itself—at any time. In President Kennedy's case there were additional factors. His popularity in and out of the United States was high. Even in those countries where he was not trusted one hundred percent, he was respected. He had begun to bring Americans together, and to a great extent had succeeded in convincing people that somehow, together, we would manage to attain a better world. He gave us hope. When he was assassinated that hope died with him, and the shocking impact of his death was accentuated by his youth and personal charm.

The effectiveness of all the mass media in reporting every aspect of the tragedy to the world is a monumental tribute to modern technology, and to the men and women of the media.

At the moment the shocking news came over the radio, I was visiting an office in which a group of people were having an informal lunch at their desks. Conversation was trivial and inconsequential. Suddenly the outer door burst open and a man from a neighboring office ran in, clutching a portable radio. His eyes were wide, and the expression on his face reflected horror mingled with disbelief. "They've shot the President!" he shouted. The enormity of his statement was such that no one believed him. But, as we crowded around him, straining to hear the breathless voice emanating from the tiny radio, the realization began to sink in. This was real. It had actually happened. Not only that, it had happened only minutes before. Of course, by this time all conception of time was suspended. However, it is not the incredible shock effect on that small, stunned group that sticks so firmly in the mind after all these years. It is something else.

The office in question was located at one of New York's busiest intersections, 42nd Street and Fifth Avenue. I will always remember looking out the window and seeing that traffic had come to a halt. Buses, trucks, taxis, and private cars were stopped. Growing clusters of pedestrians were gathered silently around stores that had radio or television sets. The usual midday roar of the city had been replaced by silence. Moments afterward, out on the street, I looked

around at the benumbed crowds milling about almost aimlessly. A long line of traffic was backed up behind a Fifth Avenue bus. The driver was weeping so hard he could not drive. All of these reactions occurred within the first half-hour after the story broke.

But even this instantaneous explosion of information and the mass reaction to it cannot compare with the incredible event that took place four days later when Jack Ruby lunged out of the crowd and shot Lee Harvey Oswald before millions of incredulous television viewers. Since the invention of motion pictures, audiences have witnessed the re-creation of violent scenes—from individual slayings to technicolor widescreen massacres. Never before, however, had a mass audience been able to witness an act of murder *as it was taking place.* To be sure we had seen the real thing before via newsreels. We had witnessed human beings being stabbed, shot, blown up, crushed, and burned to death. But, somehow, we had always been able to rationalize, telling ourselves that these horrors were not as dreadful as they seemed because, after all, what we were witnessing were only shadows of reality, moving images of darkness and light, not flesh and blood people suffering and dying. The mass media had expertly captured such occurrences and preserved them so that we could watch them after the event, cleanly and almost painlessly, at home or in the cinema. The shooting of Oswald by Ruby, seen on the television screen, however, was as great a surprise to the cameramen as to the viewers (the television crews were not there to record *that* event), and for that reason had a deeply disturbing effect unlike that of any newsreel before or since.

For the most part, mass-media coverage of major assassinations in recent years has brought credit to the media.

We must not make the mistake of blaming the carriers of bad news for the news itself. It is their duty to report. But minds are not changed as easily as one might think. People for the most part tend to read those things that reinforce their own opinions. Nevertheless, only the most rigid individuals have immutable minds.

Propagandists do take advantage of mass media to mold opinion, sometimes employing extremely subtle methods, sometimes appealing directly to the emotions. But where a free press exists they rarely go beyond this point. Experienced propagandists leave fiery rhetoric of the Black Panther, Ku Klux Klan, or Minuteman variety to those who weave ropes of their own words and then strangle on them. However, nothing can be done to prevent individuals from seizing upon an emotional situation, such as an assassination, and making use of it for partisan propaganda purposes.

When Senator Robert F. Kennedy was assassinated, no responsible Arabs, in America or abroad, expressed any satisfaction. Yet Lacey Fosburgh, in the New York *Times* of January 19, 1969, wrote:

> "The Arab community wants this trial" [that of Sirhan Sirhan], said Henry Awad, editor and publisher of the Star News and Pictorial, the largest Arab newspaper in the country. "We think it's the only way the United States will hear about the Arab cause . . . Every single Arab in America regrets the killing," Mr. Awad said, "but the trial will bring us a chance for publicity."

And in a *Times* story dated February 2, 1969, the following paragraph appeared:

> Mr. John Jabara, who was born in this country but professes strong sentiment for the Arab nationalists, said in a recent interview that he thought the most important thing that could come from the trial would be "an understanding of the Arab cause."

Any discussion of the mass media is enhanced by comments from active members of the media. A highly qualified commentator is broadcast-journalist Fred Darwin, news director of radio station WTFM, New York, and holder of the New York State Bar Association Journalism Award for constructive contributions to the administration of justice in 1965. When, for this book, the author asked for an insider's views on the relation between the mass media, assassination, and violence, he began by saying:

> Well, the first thing that occurs to me is the fact that when newsmen get together, one of the things that always come up is the enigma, couched in terms of how we cause news by covering it. The presence of the camera, which requires extra lighting and so forth, is a spotlight, and people start performing for it. In the case of demonstrations, certain violent mob action, the very presence of the camera seems to inspire action. Sometimes the directors even help. So we ask ourselves, "How can we cover news without causing it?" There is a scientific analogy. Before the electron microscope, the problem of observing things affected by light existed. How could you observe photons, for example, without changing them, because by utilizing light you changed them and made it theoretically impossible to observe their true nature.
>
> It's the same in the case of those news events that you cause by covering them, because you can also change things by not covering them. Those are the horns of the dilemma. By not covering them you can create a false climate. We've never really resolved the problem. Nobody has come up with the answer. So what we generally do is try to cover the news and hope that we won't cause too much chain reaction.

On the subject of the natural tendency of persons to imitate what they see, Mr. Darwin declared:

> We know that is a factor. We know that children who see violence on television will sometimes imitate it, just as they imitated cowboy and Indian pictures. That is one of the prices of a free press. You might say that the definition of a totalitarian

government is one in which everyone is free to agree with it. Aside from editorially disagreeing from time to time, the press must cover disagreement with the government as news. It has to cover protest. At the same time, by covering protest, it can't help but give protest a platform. It gives violence a platform. But as long as the press is not an instrument of the government it will sometimes function as an irritant to the government. It must.

On the matter of depicting violence, especially on television, Mr. Darwin said that he and his colleagues did not believe that the coverage of assassinations led to further assassinations. But he brought up a disturbing question, the enigma of "how much war, carnage, and blood we should show." Walter Cronkite of the Columbia Broadcasting System had commented on this point and said that a decision had been made to stop covering it so extensively. Apparently this was because the network executives felt that audiences were getting news coverage confused with entertainment programs about war, and they could not tell the difference between the real and the fictional. Neither Mr. Cronkite nor Mr. Darwin agrees with this. Both feel that such an attitude constitutes a dangerous underestimation of the public intelligence. Nevertheless, there are occasions when public reaction to an event reported on television news is so extreme that it becomes obvious the event itself assumed greater significance in the eyes of the public than it deserved. "If we hadn't shown so many of these extremists parading around with Viet Cong flags, burning American flags, and so forth, there wouldn't have been such a sharp reaction against such things," said Fred Darwin. These extremist acts were performed by a minority, but because a majority saw them and believed them to be of greater consequence than they were, the result was exaggeration of reality in the eyes of the audience.

Probably the greatest dilemma of a free society arises from those situations in which decision makers of the mass media exercise poor judgment while temporarily blinded by the dazzle of potentially substantial profits. What do we say about and to the publishers of a deliberately sensational book, written by an irresponsible radical advocating such illegal acts as the murder of parents, bombing of public places, and other extreme forms of violence and terrorism? When, as Mr. Darwin put it, this radical "brags about the fact that these 'establishment pigs' work to promote him and promote their own destruction to make a few dollars, he is right."

The only truly frightening aspect of the relation between the mass media and assassination and, indeed, all violence, is the "Manchurian Candidate" concept. The term comes from the title of the Richard Condon novel in which subtle brainwashing was applied to selected individuals for the purpose of assassinating a political candidate at a crucial time, thereby permitting the chosen candidate of the plotters to assume office. This may sound far-fetched, but it is a known fact that political experts believed that Senator Robert F. Kennedy had an excellent chance of being elected to the highest office in the land. During his campaign, a State Department official, who refused to permit himself to be identified and who was unavailable for questioning later by concerned reporters, made a statement that in retrospect is very ominous. Essentially he said that the businessmen of South Vietnam were far less concerned about the threat of the expected Tet offensive than they were about the threat of the candidacy of a man like Senator Kennedy.

In this age of the computer, would it not be easy for unscrupulous individuals to determine the identities of

potential assassins located in areas where the senator might make personal appearances? Would it not also be possible for those same unscrupulous individuals to subtly manipulate the media through, for example, publicity releases to the press of material specifically created to arouse potential assassins and turn them into unwitting tools? Highly unlikely, you might say. Unfortunately it is not impossible. Consider this. Proponents of the conspiracy theory in the assassination of President Kennedy have asked, "Suppose New Orleans District Attorney James Garrison really had evidence that might have led to the identification of key figures in such a conspiracy?" Would the alleged conspirators have gained anything by assassinating Garrison on the eve of whatever disclosures he claimed he was about to make? On the other hand isn't it more likely that they could have gained more by using the mass media to assassinate his character and thoroughly discredit him? Since Garrison has been largely discredited, the implications are clear.

Regardless of what theories you might hold, there is another point that must be considered. In a free society, abuses of a free press are to be expected. The danger always exists that provocative acts, legitimately covered by the mass media as news events, may trigger off extreme reactions of terrorism or assassination. Nevertheless, freedom of the press is well worth any risks involved in maintaining it.

10

OUR VIOLENT PAST and OUR UNCERTAIN FUTURE

It would be unfair to assert that the United States of America is any more liable to violence than any other nation. The entire human race has a tradition of violence, and as has been so often pointed out, *Homo sapiens* is the only species given to the slaughter of its own kind for no reason at all. Nevertheless it is difficult to avoid the conclusion that the American past was often more violent than circumstances required. Certainly our genocidal treatment of the Indians was uncalled for, and our long-standing glorification of the gunman as a hero is hardly a cause for pride. But the fact remains that many conditions in the New World were conducive to violence—so much so that only the fittest could survive.

Communications were poor. With rugged country, difficult travel conditions, and all the harsh vicissitudes imposed by living in a wilderness, those determined to remain alive did so only by adapting to the severity of their environment. Under the circumstances, adventurers had every opportunity of achieving their ends if they were hardy or unscrupulous enough. Where there was no law, and only the order imposed by nature, the man who had the most ammunition and shot straight enough was frequently the one most likely to succeed. Consequently, even those determined to live decent lives without taking advantage of others were forced to meet violence with counter violence. At least part of our violent heritage must be traced to necessity. Although good will was generally extended to strangers with more openness than today, there was also the exercise of a healthy caution toward them, and those who violated hospitality paid dearly for their indiscretions.

Dueling, though certainly not indigenous to America, was universally practiced here, despite all laws to prevent it, and the aura of romanticism surrounding it did little to discourage it. The Massachusetts law against dueling, enacted in 1719, was especially harsh. Duelists were subject to a twenty-year loss of all political rights along with ineligibility for public office. The penalty reached even beyond the grave, stating that the body of a duelist who lost his life was "appropriated to anatomical demonstration" by medical authorities.

Participation by prominent men did much to encourage dueling as the appropriate way of settling matters of honor. Unquestionably, the most famous duel in American history was the one fought by Alexander Hamilton and Aaron Burr. The political enmity between the two men was a matter of public knowledge, and though Burr was Vice President of the United States, he had been thwarted in part by the efforts of Hamilton in a bid for the New York governorship. Furthermore he knew that Hamilton had strongly opposed his vice presidency, and had influenced George Washington against awarding him a brigadier-generalship in 1798.

Burr's actual challenge came after a protracted corre-

spondence in which he demanded that Hamilton retract
a statement calling Burr "a dangerous man, and one who
ought not to be trusted with the reins of government."
The encounter was finally set for July 11, 1804, at Wee-
hawken, New Jersey. Hamilton had misgivings before the
duel, and he wrote a statement expressing his feelings
on the matter.

> *First:* My religious and moral principles are strongly opposed to
> the practice of duelling; and it would give me pain to shed the
> blood of a fellow creature in a private combat forbidden by the
> laws.

> *Secondly:* My wife and children are extremely dear to me, and
> my life is of the utmost importance to them in various views.

> *Thirdly:* I feel a sense of obligation toward my creditors, who,
> in case of accident to me, by the forced sale of my property, may
> be in some degree sufferers. I do not think myself at liberty, as a
> man of probity, lightly to expose them to hazard.

> *Fourthly:* I am conscious of no ill-will to Colonel Burr distinct
> from political opposition, which, as I trust, has proceeded from
> pure and upright motives.

> *Lastly:* I shall hazard much, and can possibly gain nothing by
> the issue of the interview.[1]

Such solid reasons notwithstanding, Hamilton went on to
say, "My *relative* situation as well in public as in private,
enforcing all the considerations which constitute what men
of the world denominate honor, imposed on me a peculiar
necessity not to decline the call."

The duel took place as arranged. Hamilton was mortally
wounded and died the following day after declaring his
forgiveness of Burr and adding that he had never intended
doing him any harm. Burr's career was ruined, and

though public opinion flared up temporarily against dueling, it was far from finished in America.

Only two years later General Andrew Jackson challenged a man named Charles Dickenson to a duel, accusing him of having repeatedly insulted Mrs. Jackson. Although the two men had discussed the matter, apparently to Jackson's satisfaction, the issue came up again, and finally the general, outraged at what he regarded as an unforgivable slight to his wife's honor, demanded satisfaction.

Dickenson, like so many well-to-do American gentlemen of the day, was as much at home with a pistol in his hand as with a walking stick. In fact, he was regarded by those who knew him as one of the best marksmen in the country. Consequently he treated Jackson's challenge lightly. The future president's friends, on the other hand, were seriously concerned about the outcome, and tried to dissuade him from going through with the affair, but he adamantly refused to listen, reminding them that he, too, was no amateur in the use of firearms.

On the day of the duel itself, May 30, 1806, Dickenson entertained his friends before going to the rendezvous by demonstrating his prowess with a pistol. There was very little doubt in their minds that he would fare well when, at twenty-odd paces, he laughingly placed four bullets in a space the size of a silver dollar. Their confidence rose even higher when, for an encore, from the same distance, he repeatedly severed a cord with bullets.

When the two adversaries finally stood facing each other, it was agreed that they would point their pistols down, wait for the signal, then raise them and fire at will. When word was given, Dickenson immediately aimed carefully and fired. A slight puff of dust seemed to fly from Jackson's coat, and his second recalled later having seen him raise his left hand and press it to his chest, but otherwise to have appeared unharmed. Dickenson, shocked, is said to have cried out, "Great God, have I missed him?" With that Jackson raised his pistol, took aim, and pulled the trigger, only to discover that the weapon was half-cocked. Pulling the hammer back with his thumb, he aimed again, fired, and mortally wounded his opponent. As Dickenson fell to the ground, Jackson's friends noticed that one of the general's shoes was covered with blood. He signaled for them to make no issue of the matter, but merely to notify Dickenson's seconds that General Jackson was satisfied. This was quickly attended to and the Jackson party hurried from the field of combat. Dickenson later died in pain, cursing to the last over the false assumption that he had missed.

Critics of Andrew Jackson have raised the point that he might have been guilty of deliberately deceiving Dickenson by wearing that particular style of loose-fitting coat, and therefore was technically guilty of premeditated murder. It is a serious accusation, but one impossible to back up after the passage of so many years. It is known that the wound troubled him until he died and may even have contributed toward his death. It hardly matters now. What this duel brings immediately to mind is a paraphrase of something Goethe once said, that men sprung from violent forefathers, will, as individuals, murderously avenge isolated acts of injury.

The practice of dueling continued to enjoy popularity in the United States until the turn of the century, to the delight of uninvolved spectators who helped perpetuate it by treating duels exactly as they would non-lethal sporting contests. It enabled the strong to kill the weak under conditions which permitted bullies to masquerade as honorable men, and it propelled fools into mortal combat over

trivial matters which could have been settled just as satis-
factorily by the toss of a coin. Southerners were especially
sensitive about their honor, and dueling south of the
Mason-Dixon line was commonplace.

In 1825, on the eve of a visit to New Orleans by the
elderly Marquis de Lafayette, a rash of duels nearly
occurred over matters of protocol and precedence in
greeting him. Had he not intervened in advance upon
hearing about these foolish quarrels, the French and
American factions of the city might have decimated each
other.

The custom of living by the gun in nineteenth-century
America made bullets the universal remedy when all other
methods of solving problems failed. Politics, being one of
the most controversial subjects, touched off especially explosive squabbles. Many were spontaneous; others were
deliberate assassination, but between an armed populace
and the ready availability of cheap whiskey, political controversies often degenerated into gun battles. Sometimes
conditions got so out of hand that bitter factional warfare
broke out.

In the early 1840's, after Texas became a republic, two
factions in Shelby County, calling themselves the Regulators and the Moderators, began bitterly disagreeing over a
number of matters. Among the chief issues were cattle
stealing, law and order, and property rights. A number
of the residents were men who had come to Texas for
reasons they preferred not to discuss; all, however, regarded the gun as supreme arbiter.

The matter of property rights was especially touchy.
Between poor record-keeping by earlier Mexican authorities, outrageous forgeries of deeds, and inadequate law
or enforcement procedures, chaos erupted. Crooked land
speculators swooped down on the area like birds of prey,

aggravating an already explosive situation. Once shooting
began between the Regulators—who took it upon themselves to do some "regulating" of the conditions they regarded as having gotten out of hand—and the Moderators
—who objected to the "regulating," and set out to "moderate" the Regulators—actual warfare erupted. The violence that ensued was so extreme that local historians
have referred to it as one of the bloodiest wars in Texas.
The conflict eventually became so severe that President
Sam Houston came to San Augustine, center of the fighting, with several companies of militia, and issued the
following proclamation:

> It having been represented to me that there exists in the county
> of Shelby a state of anarchy and misrule—that parties are arrayed
> against each other in a hostile attitude contrary to law and order—
> now, therefore, be it known, that I, Sam Houston, President of
> the Republic of Texas, to the end that hostilities may cease and
> good will and good order prevail, command all citizens engaged
> therein to lay down their arms, and retire to their respective homes.
> Given under my hand and seal,
> Sam Houston[2]

Houston did succeed in bringing about an uneasy
peace, but the two factions did not really abandon their
animosity until after Texas became a state. When the
Mexican War broke out they found a mutual enemy on
which to focus their hostilities, which were not turned in-
ward again until the 1870's. Of that period, Texas historian C. L. Douglas wrote, "It was a decade which
found its background of dissension in the program of
reconstruction which followed the war between the states
[the favorite Southern euphemism for our Civil War]; its
bloody sequences fostered by a spirit of outlawry born of
war, and of the cattle stealing troubles attendant on the
closing of the open range."[3]

There was never a greater atmosphere of hatred and violence in America than during the Civil War itself. Perhaps one of the clearest insights to at least one aspect of our violent heritage can be gained by applying a magnifying glass to the paradox that was General William Tecumseh Sherman. Southerners to this day, with ample reason, remember him with shudders, yet few Northerners or Southerners are aware that Sherman was essentially on the side of the South—at least in the beginning. After graduating from West Point he served almost exclusively at Southern posts, where he was lionized by the socially prominent. A supporter of both slavery and the doctrine of white supremacy, he finally resigned from the army, settled in Louisiana, and became head of the Louisiana Seminary of Learning and Military Academy (the predecessor of Louisiana State University). On the eve of Secession, in a letter to his brother, Senator John Sherman of Ohio, he wrote, "Practical abolition is disunion, civil war, and anarchy universal on this continent," and when the senator urged him to come back up North and re-enter government service, he replied, "I see every chance of long, confused and disorganizing civil war, and I feel no desire to take a hand therein."

When he was offered a generalship in the Confederate Army, he refused it, too, explaining that he could never perform a hostile act against the United States. Regretfully, he put all his affairs in order and departed with his family for the North under the most cordial of circumstances. What disturbed him during his homeward journey was the strong emotional tide sweeping the South, the preparations to secede and fight. He firmly rejected the right of secession, and developed an implacable bitterness against those who were breaking the bonds of Union and dragging the nation into civil war. During this period he began to experience the emotional turmoil that would eventually turn him into the first general in history to practice total war as we think of the term in the twentieth century.

In his determination to punish those he believed were destroying America, he went all out, thereby planting seeds of hatred that would outlast him and have devastating repercussions that still make themselves felt. Throughout the South he saw and felt the fierce animosity of the population toward federal troops, and he developed the theory of collective responsibility. Despite the fact that the War Department had ordered the army to leave civilians alone as long as they obeyed military authorities, Sherman decided otherwise. Thus in Mississippi and Tennessee he began to practice the systematic destruction that eventually came to be identified with him in the Southern mind. For any acts of hostility against his forces he ordered towns burned to the ground, hostages taken, and the destruction of all commodities that could not be carried off and used. This gave his army independent mobility by eliminating the need for cumbersome supply lines. It also gave the troops an unspoken license to rape, loot, and murder without fear of punishment.

Before beginning his Meridian campaign Sherman spelled out his intentions, saying, "We will take all provisions, and God help the starving families. . . ." Later, while planning his celebrated march through Georgia, he said, "Unless we can repopulate Georgia it is useless to occupy it; but in the utter destruction of its roads, houses and people, will cripple their military resources. . . . I can make the March and make Georgia howl." Paradoxically, after burning Atlanta he ended one of his communications to the city council with the following words: "But my dear sirs, when peace does come, you may call upon me for anything. Then will I share the last cracker, and watch with you to shield your homes and families against danger from any quarter."

He knew, however, that what he was doing would not be forgotten easily. In a letter to his wife he wrote:

> I doubt if history affords a parallel to the deep and bitter enmity of the women of the south . . . No one who sees them and hears them must but feel the intensity of their hate. . . . But they have sown the wind and must reap the whirlwind. Until they submit to the rightful authority of the government, they must not appeal to me for mercy or favors.

Under the circumstances, was it any wonder that future generations of Southern children would be weaned on the bitter milk of hatred for Yankees?

It was Sherman's intention ". . . to make them so sick of war that generations would pass away before they would again appeal to it." Odd as it may sound, coming from a Southern source, it was the contention of Professor E. Merton Coulter of the University of Georgia that, despite popular opinion, William T. Sherman was not a cruel man, but rather "A worshipper of the great American God, efficiency." He felt that a war should be fought and completed as quickly as possible, and by making it so horrible to those responsible for it, they would be demoralized, they would give up, and never resort to it again. "You cannot qualify war in harsher terms than I will," said Sherman. "War is cruelty, and you cannot refine it, and those who brought war into our country deserve all the curses and maledictions a people can pour out."[4]

In the aftermath of such a holocaust Americans were incapable of abandoning overnight habits and attitudes born out of war. Violence was too ingrained in the national character. The shooting was destined to continue well into the future. In addition to the personal quarrels and sectional differences that took so many lives, blood feuds broke out in border areas, raging sometimes for years. Of such protracted killing, scholar-historian J. Hubert Treston wrote:

> ". . . a single deed of blood provokes an endless series of retaliations: a hideous orgy of revenge rages through the land, an orgy which no one may escape; for old men and women and children perish, whether one by one, or in a general massacre. The vengeance is at once collective and hereditary. It strikes at neighbours and at the most distant relatives of the murderer: it strikes, too, at children that are born when the murderer has been gathered to his fathers. It ends only when there is hardly anyone left to kill, or when a paltry sum of money is offered to placate a glutted thirst for blood.[5]

Although Treston was writing specifically about the traditional unrestricted vendettas of the Balkans in *Poine, A Study in Ancient Greek Blood Vengeance,* he might just as well have been describing the infamous Hatfield-McCoy feud which lasted longer, and resulted in more deaths than any other such conflict in American history. It occurred in the Cumberland Mountain border region of Kentucky and West Virginia, where many of the inhabitants were of Scotch-Irish descent, and well aware of similar bloody feuds that touched the lives of their ancestors. The Hatfield-McCoy feud, however, had nothing to do with heritage or ancient history. It had its roots in the Civil War.

The area where this bloodshed took place is rugged, and split in two by a mountain stream called the Tug Fork. Each faction had formed armed bands during the war, ostensibly to protect local property from marauding Federal or Confederate troops. The McCoys lived in Pike County, Kentucky, and the Hatfields just across from them in West Virginia. Occasionally during the war and immediately afterward the Hatfields and the McCoys had minor disputes when one group strayed into the other's territory, but they never developed into serious fights.

The hostilities destined to reach such extreme proportions erupted in the 1870's over a foolish triviality. Floyd Hatfield, who afterward came to be known as "Hog," was accused by Randall McCoy of stealing two prized razorback hogs. Hog-stealing was a serious charge among these mountain folk, and an anonymous Kentucky circuit judge is said to have remarked once that hogs in the district seemed to have a greater value than human lives—and he was not being facetious.

To back up his accusation, Randall McCoy brought criminal charges against Floyd Hatfield. The trial was held in the hamlet of Raccoon Hollow, where the presiding magistrate happened to be "Preacher" Anse Hatfield. Members of both families attended the trial fully armed, and it came as no great surprise when McCoy lost the case. He thoroughly antagonized the Hatfields during his impassioned plea to the jury, in which he denounced the Hatfields and all their witnesses as a gang of liars and thieves. One witness, Bill Stayton, was so infuriated at McCoy's accusations that he tried to attack him in the courtroom.

The Hatfields jeered as they gloated over their victory, but the McCoys departed sullenly, threatening that the Hatfields had not heard the last of the affair. From that time on, whenever a Hatfield met a McCoy there would be a skirmish, if only a minor one. Fist fights were not especially injurious and the crude muzzle-loading rifles and cap and ball pistols they carried did little more than make loud noises whenever they shot at one another in the woods. The first blood was shed when "Devil" Anse Hatfield, brother of "Preacher" Anse, shot and killed Harmon McCoy.

But the incident that changed everything occurred one day in 1880 when Bill Stayton observed Paris and fifteen-year-old Sam McCoy approaching him in an isolated section of the woods. Knowing how they felt about him, he decided to take cover and shoot first. He waited behind a bush until they came into range, then fired, wounding Paris in the leg. McCoy returned Stayton's fire, injuring him superficially in the chest. After this exchange the two men began fighting hand to hand, punching, biting, kicking, scratching, and pummeling one another viciously. Of the two, Stayton was bigger, and Paris, weakened from the loss of blood, began getting the worst of it. Sam McCoy settled the matter by shooting Stayton dead. After Paris had rested a while the two men hid the body, but not well enough. It was discovered a few days later. Being the prime suspects, they were arrested, promptly indicted for murder, and just as promptly acquitted.

For the next two years there were no fatalities, but on election day—August 7, 1882—the Hatfields and the McCoys, along with their neighbors and friends from both sides of the state line, got drunk and quarrelsome. Old animosities flared up and serious fighting broke out. Tolbert McCoy stabbed Ellison Hatfield repeatedly, but with little success, for Hatfield threw McCoy to the ground, straddled him and was about to bash his head in with a jagged rock, when Farmer McCoy, who had been watching from the sidelines, pulled his pistol and killed Hatfield on the spot. For this, Farmer and two other McCoys were seized, held as hostages, and "executed" the next day when Ellison died.

After this, what had been sporadic violence escalated

into full-scale warfare, continuing until 1911, by which time both families were virtually wiped out. Men, women, and children had been killed for no more valid reason than bearing a name that was hateful to their slayers. Worse yet, despite the viciousness and pointlessness of the feud, it was generally regarded by participants and observers alike as a serious matter involving family honor. The neighbors, and indeed the rest of the country, gave the feud an inexcusable aura of respectability by incorporating it into folklore via story and song, to the benefit of no one and the detriment of all.

Such violent events of the past were bound to affect future generations. Do they perhaps explain, in part, at least, why we could collectively deplore atrocities in other parts of the world, while tolerating them at home? While we decried the brutal acts of political murderers in Germany, Italy, and Russia, our indigenous counterparts performed parallel deeds. In 1930, James Irwin, of Ocilla, Georgia, was tried and convicted of murder. Had he not been black it is unlikely that he would have died in such barbaric style. Dragged from his jail cell at night by a cursing, angry mob, he was taken to a wooded area, shackled to a tree, subjected to prolonged physical torture, then doused with gasoline, and set afire to serve as a blazing target for the benefit of those present who felt impelled to engage in pistol practice. How accurate were the words of Major General Sir Charles James Napier, C.B., who wrote of Americans a century earlier, "Lord deliver us from republics where enslaved Negroes are roasted alive." And how prophetic the verse of the anonymous eighteenth-century poet, who predicted:

> Some Afric Chief will rise, who scorns chains,
> Racks, tortures, flames, excruciating pains,
> Will lead his injur'd friends to bloody fight,

And in the flooded carnage take delight;
Then dear repay us in some vengeful war,
And give us blood for blood, scar for scar.[6]

The unrest, the violence, and, certainly, the assassinations of the 1960's and of 1970 did not erupt spontaneously. Such conditions have been fermenting in some cases since the birth of the United States. The genius of the founding fathers provided us with a system that has, so far, withstood all efforts to tear it apart. But it was not without flaws. Benjamin Franklin recognized one, arguing vainly for an anti-slavery clause in the original draft of the Constitution, predicting, when his proposal was defeated, that without it the country could not last two hundred years. His prediction took on terrible significance when the Civil War broke out, but the nation did survive. With the Declaration of Independence as a starting point, however, Ben Franklin's deadline does not come upon us until 1976.

Fear, frustration, and concern about the future of a strife-torn, overcrowded, and ailing planet do not bode well for the future. Violence has not subsided to any extent anywhere, because when the flames die down in one place they blaze up again elsewhere. Extremism rocks society the world over, even in the United States, where most Americans once shared the opinion of Thomas Paine, who said:

You will do me the justice to remember, that I have always strenuously supported the right of every man to his opinion, however different that opinion may be to mine. He who denies to another this right, makes a slave of himself to his present opinion, because he precludes himself the right of changing it. The most formidable weapon against errors of every kind is reason. I have never used any other, and I trust I never shall.[7]

It is when all reason is abandoned that society is in gravest danger, for when reason gives way to violent action all men suffer.

Whether violence will increase or decrease in the future depends on the ability, not only of Americans, but of the entire human race, to adapt to change smoothly, and to abandon all attitudes that intrinsically hinder harmony and progress. World leaders have been debating the subject of disarmament since the Prophet Isaiah conceived of beating swords into plowshares and spears into pruning hooks. As long as individuals arm themselves in hatred and fear, governments—which, in the final analysis, are nothing more than groups of individuals with access to bigger, more destructive weapons—can hardly be expected to behave differently.

In other areas, increasing social pressures are squeezing ordinary people to the limits of endurance. A Stanford University professor of psychology, Philip G. Zimbardo, was most specific about the problem. After conducting a series of laboratory experiments dealing with anonymity and aggression coupled with field studies on vandalism among white middle-class Americans, he theorized that we are being turned by conditions into potential assassins. Calling upon an impressive array of data, Dr. Zimbardo indicated the sharp increase of homicide in the late 1960's; he estimated that approximately 40,000 children are annually beaten or tortured by members of their own families; and he pointed out that between 1963 and 1969 alone there had been 250 violent outbreaks of urban violence, not to mention the assassinations of Medgar Evers, Malcolm X, the Reverend Martin Luther King, Jr., President John F. Kennedy, and Senator Robert F. Kennedy.

On the subject of vandalism, Dr. Zimbardo revealed that

in 1967 alone, vandals in New York had smashed 202,712 school windows, 360,000 pay telephones, damaged $100,000 worth of transit property, and $750,000 worth of city park property. "What we are observing around us, then," he wrote, "is a sudden change in the restraints which normally control the expression of our drives, impulses, and emotions." His paper, which was presented to the Nebraska Symposium on Motivation at the University of Nebraska, in March 1969, was based not only on his own experiments, but on historical, anthropological, psychological, and psychiatric observations of other social scientists. He declared that a process which he termed "deindividuation" was setting in, a process which arose from factors such as increased feelings of anonymity among city dwellers, and a watering-down of social responsibility on their part. Size of cities, he said, increased feelings of powerlessness in individuals, and such diverse factors as rootlessness and mobility were contributing toward a general weakening of restraints growing out of self-evaluation. "Conditions which foster deindividuation," he declared, "make each of us a potential assassin."[8]

A potential assassin, however, does not assume the label until the potential has been realized. But as long as a climate which nourishes potential assassins is permitted to exist, then society will never be safe from their attacks. If modern nihilists, euphemistically calling themselves revolutionaries, go too far, they may succeed only in reaping a whirlwind far more devastating than the one visualized by General Sherman, and one that could engulf us all.

Among us there are also rational men who are not regarded as extremists, nihilists, or even revolutionaries in the true sense of the word. They are the most frightening men of all. Not only do they advocate tyrannicide in the classic sense, but they go beyond it and seriously advocate assassination as an alternative to war. It is the belief of such theorists that if countless lives can be saved by avoiding war through the assassination of national leaders, "it is vitally important to face the fact that, where the methods of ridding ourselves of these doers of dirty work, evolved by social and political scientists from Aristotle to Marx, fail, we have literally no recourse but assassination, and today this truth has become much more important than ever in man's history."[9]

So wrote Edward Hyams in 1969. What makes his theory so frightening is not that he may be right, but that there are those who, in agreeing with him, might do something to change theory into reality. The questions Hyams did not answer were vital:

(1) Who decides what leader's death will avert war?

and

(2) What happens in the event of a miscalculation?

The answers, though slightly indirect, may be found between the lines of quotes from two controversial thinkers, Voltaire and Freud. "It is forbidden to kill," said Voltaire, "therefore all murderers are punished unless they kill in large numbers and to the sound of trumpets."[10] The less cynical, but pragmatic Freud went a step further, saying, "The very emphasis of the commandment: Thou shalt not kill, makes it certain that we are descended from an endless chain of murderers, whose love of murder was in their blood as it is perhaps in ours."[11]

It is up to future generations to prove or disprove these words.

DOCUMENTS

INTRODUCTORY NOTE—DOCUMENT I

As the first Westerner to write about the Assassins, Marco Polo deserves special attention. The following excerpt is from Book I of the celebrated Venetian's travel memoir, and includes three short chapters containing his account of "The Old Man of the Mountain." The translation is one of the most interesting ever made, primarily because of the scholarship of the translator, Colonel Sir Henry Yule, R.E., C.B., K.C.S.I. His footnotes are left intact here in order to convey to the modern reader the extreme lengths to which the scholar-adventurers of his breed went in their pursuit of knowledge. The excerpts are from the third revised translation which was published by Charles Scribner's Sons, New York, in 1903.

CHAPTER XXIII

Concerning the Old Man of the Mountain

Mulehet is a country in which the Old Man of the Mountain dwelt in former days; and the name means *"Place of the Aram."* I will tell you his whole history as related by Messer Marco Polo, who heard it from several natives of that region.

The Old Man was called in their language Aloadin. He had caused a certain valley between two mountains to be enclosed, and had turned it into a garden, the largest and most beautiful that ever was seen, filled with every variety of fruit. In it were erected pavilions and palaces the most elegant that can be imagined, all covered with gilding and exquisite painting. And there were runnels too, flowing freely with wine and milk and honey and water; and numbers of ladies and of the most beautiful damsels in the world, who could play on all manner of instruments, and sung most sweetly, and danced in a manner that it was charming to behold. For the Old Man desired to make his people believe that this was actually Paradise. So he had fashioned it after the description that Mahommet gave of his Paradise, to wit, that it should be a beautiful garden running with conduits of wine and milk and honey and water, and full of lovely women for the delectation of all its inmates. And sure enough the Saracens of those parts believed that it *was* Paradise!

Now no man was allowed to enter the Garden save those whom he intended to be his ASHISHIN. There was a Fortress at the entrance to the Garden, strong enough to resist all the world, and there was no other way to get in. He kept at his Court a number of the youths of the country, from 12 to 20 years of age, such as had a taste for soldiering, and to these he used to tell tales about Paradise, just as Mahommet had been wont to do, and they believed in him just as the Saracens believe in Mahommet. Then he would introduce them into his garden, some four, or six, or ten at a time, having first made them drink a certain potion which cast them into a deep sleep, and then causing them to be lifted and carried in. So when they awoke, they found themselves in the Garden.[1]

NOTE I.—Says the venerable Sire de Joinville: *"Le Vieil de la Montaingne ne crèoit pas en Mahommet, ainçois crèoit en la Loi de*

Haali, qui fu Oncle Mahommet." This is a crude statement, no doubt, but it has a germ of truth. Adherents of the family of Ali as the true successors of the Prophet existed from the tragical day of the death of Husain, and among these, probably owing to the secrecy with which they were compelled to hold their allegiance, there was always a tendency to all manner of strange and mystical doctrines; as in one direction to the glorification of Ali as a kind of incarnation of the Divinity, a character in which his lineal representatives were held in some manner to partake; in another direction to the development of Pantheism, and release from all positive creed and precepts. Of these Aliites, eventually called *Shiâhs,* a chief sect, and parent of many heretical branches, were the Ismailites, who took their name, from the seventh Imam, whose return to earth they professed to expect at the end of the World. About A.D. 1090 a branch of the Ismaili stock was established by Hassan, son of Sabah, in the mountainous districts of Northern Persia; and, before their suppression by the Mongols, 170 years later, the power of the quasi-spiritual dynasty which Hassan founded had spread over the Eastern Kohistan, at least as far as Káïn. Their headquarters were at Alamút ("Eagle's Nest"), about 32 miles north-east of Kazwin, and all over the territory which they held they established fortresses of great strength. De Sacy seems to have proved that they were called *Hashishíya* or *Hashishín,* from their use of the preparation of hemp called *Hashish;* and thence, through their system of murder and terrorism, came the modern application of the word Assassin. The original aim of this system was perhaps that of a kind of *Vehmgericht,* to punish or terrify orthodox persecutors who were too strong to be faced with the sword. I have adopted in the text one of the readings of the G. Text *Asciscin,* as expressing the original word with the greatest accuracy that Italian spelling admits. In another author we find it as *Chazisii* (see *Bollandists,* May, vol. ii. p. xi.); Joinville calls them *Assacis;* whilst Nangis and others corrupt the name into *Harsacidae,* and what not.

The explanation of the name MULEHET as it is in Ramusio, or *Mulcete* as it is in the G. Text (the last expressing in Rusticiano's Pisan tongue the strongly aspirated *Mulhĕtĕ*), is given by the former: "This name of Mulehet is as much as to say in the Saracen tongue *'The Abode of Heretics,' "* the fact being that it does represent the Arabic term *Mulhid,* pl. *Mulâhidah,* "Impii, heretici," which is in the

Persian histories (as of Rashíduddín and Wassáf) the title most commonly used to indicate this community, and which is still applied by orthodox Mahomedans to the Nosairis, Druses, and other sects of that kind, more or less kindred to the Ismaili. The writer of the *Tabakat-i-Násiri* calls the sectarians of Alamút *Muláhidat-ul-maut,* "Heretics of Death." The curious reading of the G. Text which we have preserved *"vaut à dire des* Aram," should be read as we have rendered it. I conceive that Marco was here unconsciously using one Oriental term to explain another. For it seems possible to explain *Aram* only as standing for *Harám,* in the sense of "wicked" or "reprobate."

In Pauthier's Text, instead of *des aram,* we find *"veult dire en françois* Diex Terrien," or Terrestrial God. This may have been substituted, in the correction of the original rough dictation, from a perception that the first expression was unintelligible. The new phrase does not indeed convey the meaning of *Muláhidah,* but it expresses a main characteristic of the heretical doctrine. The correction was probably made by Polo himself; it is certainly of very early date. For in the romance of Bauduin de Sebourc, which I believe dates early in the 14th century, the Caliph, on witnessing the extraordinary devotion of the followers of the Old Man (see note I, ch. xxiv.), exclaims:

> "Par Mahon . . . .
> Vous estes *Diex en terre,* autre coze n'i a!"

So also Fr. Jacopo d'Aqui in the *Imago Mundi,* says of the Assassins: "Dicitur iis quod sunt in Paradiso magno *Dei Terreni"*—expressions, no doubt, taken in both cases from Polo's book.

Khanikoff, and before him J. R. Forster, have supposed that the name *Mulehet* represents *Alamút.* But the resemblance is much closer and more satisfactory to *Mulhid* or *Muláhidah. Mulhet* is precisely the name by which the kingdom of the Ismailites is mentioned in Armenian history, and *Mulihet* is already applied in the same way by Rabbi Benjamin in the 12th century, and by Rubruquis in the 13th. The Chinese narrative of Hulaku's expedition calls it the kingdom of *Mulahi. (Joinville,* p. 138; *J. As.* sér. II., tom. xii. 285; *Benj. Tudela,* p. 106; *Rub.* p. 265; *Rémusat, Nouv. Mélanges,* I. 176; *Gaubil,* p. 128; *Pauthier,* pp. cxxxix.–cxli.; *Mon. Hist. Patr. Scriptorum,* III. 1559, Turin, 1848.)

"Old Man of the Mountain" was the title applied by the Crusaders to the chief of that branch of the sect which was settled in the mountains north of Lebanon, being a translation of his popular Arabic title *Shaikh-ul-Jibal*. But according to Hammer this title properly belonged, as Polo gives it, to the Prince of Alamút, who never called himself Sultan, Malik, or Amir; and this seems probable, as his territory was known as the *Balad-ul-Jibal*.

CHAPTER XXIV

How the Old Man used to train his Assassins

When therefore they awoke, and found themselves in a place so charming, they deemed that it was Paradise in very truth. And the ladies and damsels dallied with them to their hearts' content, so that they had what young men would have; and with their own good will they never would have quitted the place.

Now this Prince whom we call the Old One kept his Court in grand and noble style, and made those simple hill-folks about him believe firmly that he was a great Prophet. And when he wanted one of his *Ashishin* to send on any mission, he would cause that potion whereof I spoke to be given to one of the youths in the garden, and then had him carried into his Palace. So when the young man awoke, he found himself in the Castle, and no longer in that Paradise; whereat he was not over well pleased. He was then conducted to the Old Man's presence, and bowed before him with great veneration as believing himself to be in the presence of a true Prophet. The Prince would then ask whence he came, and he would reply that he came from Paradise! and that it was exactly such as Mahommet had described it in the Law. This of course gave the others who stood by, and who had not been admitted, the greatest desire to enter therein.

So when the Old Man would have any Prince slain, he would say to such a youth: "Go thou and slay So and So; and when thou returnest my Angels shall bear thee into Paradise. And shouldst thou die, natheless even so will I send my Angels to carry thee back into Paradise." So he caused them to believe; and thus there was no order of his that they would not affront any peril to execute, for the great desire they had to get back into that Paradise of his. And in this manner the Old One got his people to murder any one whom he desired to get rid of. Thus, too, the great dread that he inspired all Princes withal, made them become his tributaries in order that he might abide at peace and amity with them.[1]

I should also tell you that the Old Man had certain others under him, who copied his proceedings and acted exactly in the same manner. One of these was sent into the territory of Damascus, and the other into Curdistan.[2]

NOTE I.—Romantic as this story is, it seems to be precisely the same that was current over all the East. It is given by Odoric at length, more briefly by a Chinese author, and again from an Arabic source by Hammer in the *Mines de l'Orient*.

The following is the Chinese account as rendered by Rémusat: "The soldiers of this country (Mulahi) are veritable brigands. When they see a lusty youth, they tempt him with the hope of gain, and bring him to such a point that he will be ready to kill his father or his elder brother with his own hand. After he is enlisted, they intoxicate him, and carry him in that state into a secluded retreat, where he is charmed with delicious music and beautiful women. All his desires are satisfied for several days, and then (in sleep) he is transported back to his original position. When he awakes, they ask what he has seen. He is then informed that if he will become an Assassin, he will be rewarded with the same felicity. And with the texts and prayers that they teach him they heat him to such a pitch that whatever commission be given him he will brave death without regret in order to execute it."

The Arabic narrative is too long to extract. It is from a kind of historical romance called *The Memoirs of Hakim,* the date of which Hammer unfortunately omits to give. Its close coincidence in substance with Polo's story is quite remarkable. After a detailed description of the Paradise, and the transfer into it of the aspirant under the influence of *bang,* on his awaking and seeing his chief enter, he says, "O chief! am I awake or am I dreaming?" To which the chief: "O such an One, take heed that thou tell not the dream to any stranger. Know that Ali thy Lord hath vouchsafed to show thee the place destined for thee in Paradise. . . . Hesitate not a moment therefore in the service of the Imam who thus deigns to intimate his contentment with thee," and so on.

William de Nangis thus speaks of the Syrian Shaikh, who alone was known to the Crusaders, though one of their historians (*Jacques de Vitry,* in *Bongars,* I. 1062) shows knowledge that the headquarters of the sect was in Persia: "He was much dreaded far and near, by both Saracens and Christians, because he so often caused princes of both classes indifferently to be murdered by his emissaries. For he used to bring up in his palace youths belonging to his territory, and had them taught a variety of languages, and above all things to fear their Lord and obey him unto death, which would thus become to them an entrance into the joys of Paradise. And whosoever of them thus perished in carrying out his Lord's behests was worshipped as an angel." As an instance of the implicit obedience rendered by the *Fidáwí* or devoted disciples of the Shaikh, Fra Pipino and Marino Sanuto relate that when Henry Count of Champagne (titular King of Jerusalem) was on a visit to the Old Man of Syria, one day as they walked together they saw some lads in white sitting on the top of a high tower. The Shaikh, turning to the Count, asked if he had any subjects as obedient as his own? and without giving time for reply made a sign to two of the boys, who immediately leapt from the tower, and were killed on the spot. The same story is told in the

Cento Novelle Antiche, as happening when the Emperor Frederic was on a visit (imaginary) to the Veglio. And it is introduced likewise as an incident in the Romance of Bauduin de Sebourc:

> "Vollés veioir merveilles? dist li Rois Seignouris"

to Bauduin and his friends, and on their assenting he makes the signal to one of his men on the battlements, and in a twinkling

> "Quant le vinrent en l'air salant de tel avis,
> Et aussi liément, et aussi esjois,
> Qu'il deust conquester mil livres de parisis!
> Ains qu'il venist a tière il fut mors et fenis,
> Surles roches agues desrompis corps et pis,"* etc.

(*Cathay,* 153; *Rémusat, Nouv. Mél.* I. 178; *Mines de l'Orient, III.* 201 *seqq.; Nangis* in *Duchesne,* V. 332; *Pipino* in *Muratori,* IX. 705: *Defrémery* in *J. As.* sér. V. tom. v. 34 *seqq.; Cent. Nov. Antiche,* Firenze, 1572, p. 91; *Bauduin de Sebourc,* I. 359.)

The following are some of the more notable murders or attempts at murder ascribed to the Ismailite emissaries either from Syria or from Persia:—

A.D. 1092. Nizum-ul-Mulk, formerly the powerful minister of Malik Shah, Seljukian sovereign of Persia, and a little later his two sons. 1102. The Prince of Homs, in the chief Mosque of that city. 1113. Maudúd, Prince of Mosul, in the chief Mosque of Damascus. About 1114. Abul Muzafar 'Ali, Wazir of Sanjár Shah, and Chakar Beg, grand-uncle of the latter. 1116. Ahmed Yel, Prince of Maragha, at Baghdad, in the presence of Mahomed, Sultan of Persia. 1121. The Amir Afdhal, the powerful Wazir of Egypt, at Cairo. 1126. Kasim Aksonkor, Prince of Mosul and Aleppo, in the Great Mosque at Mosul. 1127. Moyin-uddin, Wazir of Sanjár Shah of Persia. 1129. Amír Billah, Khalif of Egypt. 1131. Taj-ul Mulúk Buri, Prince of Damascus. 1134. Shams-ul-Mulúk, son of the preceding. 1135-38. The Khalif Mostarshid, the Khalif Rashíd, and Daùd, Seljukian Prince of Azerbaijan. 1149. Raymond, Count of Tripoli. 1191. Kizil Arzlan,

---

* This story has been transferred to Peter the Great, who is alleged to have exhibited the docility of his subjects in the same way to the King of Denmark, by ordering a Cossack to jump from the Round Tower at Copenhagen, on the summit of which they were standing.

Prince of Azerbaijan. 1192. Conrad of Montferrat, titular King of Jerusalem; a murder which King Richard has been accused of instigating. 1217. Oghulmish, Prince of Hamadán.

And in 1174 and 1176 attempts to murder the great Saladin. 1271. Attempt to murder Ala'uddin Juwaini, Governor of Baghdad, and historian of the Mongols. 1272. The attempt to murder Prince Edward of England at Acre.

In latter years the *Fidáwi* or Ismailite adepts appear to have let out their services simply as hired assassins. Bibars, in a letter to his court at Cairo, boasts of using them when needful. A Mahomedan author ascribes to Bibars the instigation of the attempt on Prince Edward.

NOTE 2.—Hammer mentions as what he chooses to call "Grand Priors" under the Shaikh or "Grand Master" at Alamút, the chief, in Syria, one in the Kuhistan of E. Persia (Tun-o-Kaïn), one in Kumis (the country about Damghan and Bostam), and one in Irák; he does not speak of any in Kurdistan. Colonel Monteith, however, says, though without stating authority or particulars, "There were several divisions of them (the Assassins) scattered throughout Syria, *Kurdistan* (near the Lake of Wan), and Asia Minor, but all acknowledging as Imaum or High Priest the Chief residing at Alamut." And it may be noted that Odoric, a generation after Polo, puts the Old Man at *Millescorte,* which looks like *Malasgird,* north of Lake Van.

CHAPTER XXV

HOW THE OLD MAN CAME BY HIS END

Now it came to pass, in the year of Christ's Incarnation, 1252, that Alaü, Lord of the Tartars of the Levant, heard tell of these great crimes of the Old Man, and resolved to make an end of him. So he took and sent one of his Barons with a great Army to that Castle, and they besieged it for three years, but they could not take it, so strong was it. And indeed if they had had food within it

never would have been taken. But after being besieged
those three years they ran short of victual, and were
taken. The Old Man was put to death with all his men
[and the Castle with its Garden of Paradise was levelled
with the ground]. And since that time he has had no
successor; and there was an end to all his villainies.[1]

NOTE 1.—The date in Pauthier is 1242; in the G. T. and in Ramusio
1262. Neither is right, nor certainly could Polo have meant the former.

When Mangku Kaan, after his enthronement (1251), determined at
a great *Kurultai* or Diet, on perfecting the Mongol conquests, he
entrusted his brother Kúbláï with the completion of the subjugation
of China and the adjacent countries, whilst his brother Hulaku received the command of the army destined for Persia and Syria. The
complaints that came from the Mongol officers already in Persia determined him to commence with the reduction of the Ismailites, and
Hulaku set out from Karakorum in February, 1254. He proceeded
with great deliberation, and the Oxus was not crossed till January,
1256. But an army had been sent long in advance under "one of his
Barons," Kitubuka Noyan, and in 1253 it was already actively engaged in besieging the Ismailite fortresses. In 1255, during the progress
of the war, ALA'UDDIN MAHOMED, the reigning Prince of the Assassins
(mentioned by Polo as Alaodin), was murdered at the instigation of
his son Ruknuddin Khurshah, who succeeded to the authority. A
year later (November, 1256) Ruknuddin surrendered to Hulaku.
[Bretschneider (*Med. Res.* II. p. 109) says that Alamút was taken by
Hulaku, 20th December, 1256.—H. C.] The fortresses given up, all
well furnished with provisions and artillery engines, were 100 in
number. Two of them, however, Lembeser and Girdkuh, refused to
surrender. The former fell after a year; the latter is stated to have
held out for *twenty years*—actually, as it would seem, about fourteen,
or till December, 1270. Ruknuddin was well treated by Hulaku, and
despatched to the Court of the Kaan. The accounts of his death differ,
but that most commonly alleged, according to Rashiduddin, is that
Mangku Kaan was irritated at hearing of his approach, asking why
his post-horses should be fagged to no purpose, and sent executioners
to put Ruknuddin to death on the road. Alamút had been surrendered
without any substantial resistance. Some survivors of the sect got hold

of it again in 1275-1276, and held out for a time. The dominion was extinguished, but the sect remained, though scattered indeed and obscure. A very strange case that came before Sir Joseph Arnould in the High Court at Bombay in 1866 threw much new light on the survival of the Ismailis.

Some centuries ago a *Dai* or Missionary of the Ismailis, named Sadruddín, made converts from the Hindu trading classes in Upper Sind. Under the name of *Khojas* the sect multiplied considerably in Sind, Kach'h, and Guzerat, whence they spread to Bombay and to Zanzibar. Their numbers in Western India are now probably not less than 50,000 to 60,000. Their doctrine, or at least the books which they revere, appear to embrace a strange jumble of Hindu notions with Mahomedan practices and Shiah mysticism, but the main characteristic endures of deep reverence, if not worship, of the person of their hereditary Imám. To his presence, when he resided in Persia, numbers of pilgrims used to betake themselves, and large remittances of what we may call *Ismail's Pence* were made to him. Abul Hassan, the last Imám but one of admitted lineal descent from the later Shaikhs of Alamút, and claiming (as they did) descent from the Imám Ismail and his great ancestor 'Ali Abu Tálib, had considerable estates at Meheláti, between Kúm and Hamadán, and at one time held the Government of Kermán. His son and successor, Shah Khalilullah, was killed in a brawl at Yezd in 1818. Fatteh 'Ali Sháh, fearing Ismailite vengeance, caused the homicide to be severely punished, and conferred gifts and honours on the young Imám, Agha Khan, including the hand of one of his own daughters. In 1840 Agha Khan, who had raised a revolt at Kermán, had to escape from Persia. He took refuge in Sind, and eventually rendered good service both to General Nott at Kandahár and to Sir C. Napier in Sind, for which he receives a pension from our Government.

For many years this genuine Heir and successor of the *Viex de la Montaingne* has had his headquarters at Bombay, where he devotes, or for a long time did devote, the large income that he receives from the faithful to the maintenance of a racing stable, being the chief patron and promoter of the Bombay Turf!

A schism among the Khojas, owing apparently to the desire of part of the well-to-do Bombay community to sever themselves from the peculiarities of the sect and to set up as respectable Sunnis, led in 1866 to an action in the High Court, the object of which was to exclude Agha Khan from all rights over the Khojas, and to transfer the property of the community to the charge of Orthodox Mahomedans. To the elaborate addresses of Mr. Howard and Sir Joseph Arnould, on this most singular process before an English Court, I owe the preceding particulars. The judgment was entirely in favour of the Old Man of the Mountain.

[Sir Bartle Frere writes of Agha Khan in 1875: "Like his ancestor, the Old One of Marco Polo's time, he keeps his court in grand and noble style. His sons, popularly known as 'The Persian Princes,' are active sportsmen, and age has not dulled the Agha's enjoyment of horse-racing. Some of the best blood of Arabia is always to be found in his stables. He spares no expense on his racers, and no prejudice of religion or race prevents his availing himself of the science and skill of an English trainer or jockey when the races come round. If tidings of war or threatened disturbance should arise from Central Asia or Persia, the Agha is always one of the first to hear of it, and seldom fails to pay a visit to the Governor or to some old friend high in office to hear the news and offer the services of a tried sword and an experienced leader to the Government which has so long secured him a quiet refuge for his old age." Agha Khan died in April, 1881, at the age of 81. He was succeeded by his son Agha Ali Sháh, one of the members of the Legislative Council. (See *The Homeward Mail, Overland Times of India,* of 14th April, 1881.)]

The *Bohras* of Western India are identified with the Imámí-Ismáilís in some books, and were so spoken of in the first edition of this work. This is, however, an error, originally due, it would seem, to Sir John Malcolm. The nature of their doctrine, indeed, seems to be very much alike, and the Bohras, like the Ismáilís, attach a divine character to their *Mullah* or chief pontiff, and make a pilgrimage to his presence once in life. But the *persons* so reverenced are quite different; and the Bohras recognise all the 12 Imáms of ordinary Shiahs. Their first appearance in India was early, the date which they assign being A.H. 532 (A.D. 1137–1138). Their chief seat was in Yemen, from which a large emigration to India took place on its conquest by the Turks in 1538. Ibn Batuta seems to have met with Bohras at Gandár, near Baroch, in 1342. (*Voyages,* IV. 58.)

A Chinese account of the expedition of Hulaku will be found in Rémusat's *Nouveaux Mélanges* (I.), and in Pauthier's Introduction.

(*Q. R.* 115-219, esp. 213; *Ilch.* vol. i; *J. A. S. B.* VI. 842 *seqq.*) [A new and complete translation has been given by Dr. E. Bretschneider, *Med. Res.* I. 112 *seqq.* —H. C.]

There is some account of the rock of Alamút and its exceedingly slender traces of occupancy, by Colonel Monteith, in *J. R. G. S.* III. 15, and again by Sir Justin Sheil in vol. viii. p. 431. There does not seem to be any specific authority for assigning the Paradise of the Shaikh to Alamút; and it is at least worthy of note that another of the castles of the Muláhidah, destroyed by Hulaku, was called *Firdús, i.e.* Paradise. In any case, I see no reason to suppose that Polo visited Alamút, which would have been quite out of the road that he is following.

It is possible that "the Castle," to which he alludes at the beginning of next chapter, and which set him off upon this digression, was *Girdkuh.** It has not, as far as I know, been identified by modern travellers, but it stood within 10 or 12 miles of Damghan (to the west or north-west). It is probably the *Tigado* of Hayton, of which he thus speaks: "The Assassins had an impregnable castle called Tigado, which was furnished with all necessaries, and was so strong that it had no fear of attack on any side. Howbeit, Haloön commanded a certain captain of his that he should take 10,000 Tartars who had been left in garrison in Persia, and with them lay siege to the said castle, and not leave it till he had taken it. Wherefore the said Tartars continued besieging it for seven whole years, winter and summer, without being able to take it. At last the Assassins surrendered, from sheer want of clothing, but not of victuals or other necessaries." So Ramusio; other copies read "27 years." In any case it corroborates the fact that Girdkuh was said to have held out for an extraordinary length of time. If Rashiduddin is right in naming 1270 as the date of surrender, this would be quite a recent event when the Polo party passed, and draw special attention to the spot. (*J. As.* sér. IV. tom. xiii. 48; *Ilch.* I. 93, 104, 274; *Q. R.* p. 278; *Ritter,* VIII. 336.) A note which I have from *Djihan Numa* (I. 259) connects Girdkuh with a district called *Chinar.* This may be a clue to the term *Arbre Sec;* but there are difficulties.

---

* [Girdkuh means "round mountain"; it was in the district of Kumis, three parasangs west of Damghan. Under the year 1257, the *Yüan shi* mentions the taking of the fortress of *Ghi-rh-du-kie* by *K'ie-di-bu-hua.* (*Bretschneider, Med. Res.* I. p. 122; II. 110.)—H. C.]

INTRODUCTORY NOTE—DOCUMENT II

In that Louis J. Wiechmann was one of the principal witnesses at the Lincoln assassination conspirators' trial, and the man who reported the existence of a conspiracy long before the assassination occurred, his official statement to the police afterward is highly significant. It is taken from the National Archives, War Department Records File "W" R.B., JAO, page 99.

Wiechmann's Initial Police Statement

Met Herold three times in his life. First time at Mrs. Surratt's in '63. Last time eight or ten weeks ago.

Surrat (*sic*) studied divinity. Was in Express Office in this city in January. It was on Good Friday that I went with Mrs. Surratt to the county—Surratsville. She gave me ten dollars with which to hire horse. Nothe was the man who owed her money. Gwinn was her agent. Noff was present. Started from here about half-past two; got there about four; remained until half-past six. Did not eat; drank port wine sangaree. Left there at 6½; got back here at half-past nine; retired about ten o'clock. Hired the horse from Brooks on G Street. Surrat left the house with a woman by name of Slater, March 27th. Came back on the 3 of April. Had nine or eleven pieces of gold. Hollohan boarded there. I had been there, at Surrattsville, with Mrs. Surratt, on the Tuesday previous to Good Friday—same week Mrs. Surrat told me to go and get Booth's buggy. Booth had sold the buggy, but gave me ten dollars to hire one with.

Left at 9; arrived at 12. Roads muddy. Stayed 15 minutes. She went on to Gwinn's house; took dinner; drove up to Surrattsville with Gwinn. Saw Nothe there. Got back here about 8 o'clock. Nothe, Gwinn and Mrs. Surratt in the parlor. Drove there once in March 1864. First time Mrs. Surratt took a basket with food in it—cakes. Next time a package which she said contained china dishes—a round package—6 or 8 inches in diameter.

I made Booth's acquaintance on same day that Surratt did—on the 15th of Jan. last. Dr. Mudd introduced Booth to us both. Booth called Mudd and Surratt out and had private conversation with them. Drew something on back of envelope—did not seem to be writing. Met Booth frequently at Mrs. Surratt's. Surratt and Booth used to have private interviews. Met Booth at Mrs. S.'s at the hotel; walked down 7th Street; over and at restaurant near Ford's theatre. Atzerodt, Harold and Surratt were all there; also Hollohan. Went from there to Hollohan's. Time Booth played his last piece, he played for the benefit of McCulloch. After 4th of March wrote to Bishop McGill, at Richmond, Oct. 27th, 1864, and March 15th, 1864. Received reply from him. Shows Sec'y. Booth was at Mrs. Surratt's house at half-past two o'clock on day of the assassination.

Surratt came to me once to have me write something flowery about Booth's having withdrawn from the stage and become speculator. Surratt said he had taken twenty shares in oil himself; that Booth had made $10,000. I have had discussions on politics. Lady hit me over the head with brush—Mrs. Surratt. It was about slavery and our soldiers. Mad because I went down stairs with blue pants on. Paine has been at the house twice; first time ten weeks ago. Enquired for Mr. Surratt—out. I invited him in. He said his name was Wood. He came again, and second time gave his name as Paine. Said he had been in the South, but had come North and taken the oath. Stayed there three days. Found false mustache in my room. Went upstairs in third story and found Surratt and Paine playing with bowie knives. Also saw two revolves (*sic*) and five setts & pins.

Miss Anna Ward; had no doubt spoken to her. Miss Mary Murray: Keeps Herndon House. Met Atzerodt. He said, "Have you seen Paine?" I said "No; is he at the Herndon House?" He said "Yes." On night of April 18th left Porterfield's house in ———. Have seen two letters from Surratt. One to his mother, and the other to Miss Ward. The one to his mother was dated April 12th; that to Miss Ward, ——— Anna Ward is teacher at convent on corner of 10th and G. Streets. Saw telegram from Booth. It read: "Telegraph John number and street at once."

Mrs. Slater is a blockade runner. Learned from Mrs. Surratt that she and Surratt had gone to Richmond on March 27, 1865. Hollohan has seen her at the house twice. I saw her but once; always had her veil down. A man by the name of Howell was there in the beginning of February. Think him a blockade runner. Mrs. Surratt said he was. His movements about the house were suspicious; would not go out nights. Saw Surratt last on April 3d. Took oysters with him. Said he saw Benjamin and Davis, and they said Richmond would not be evacuated. Had been bad and dissipated for some time; had been in house of ill-fame.

Mrs. Surratt made the remark, —"a funny looking preacher," as to Paine. J. H. Surratt is 21 years of age. Think he went once to Richmond in March, '64. Told me by route of Baltimore. Joseph Surratt, living in Steubenville, is a cousin to Anna Surratt. Told Capt. Gleason my suspicions several weeks ago.

INTRODUCTORY NOTE—DOCUMENT III

The fact that Major Henry R. Rathbone was sitting in the box at Ford's Theater when Abraham Lincoln was shot, and that he grappled with John Wilkes Booth immediately afterward made him the most important eyewitness to the crime. His official statement, therefore, is of prime historical importance. A tragic footnote to the life of Major Rathbone is the story of his end. Some time after his marriage to Miss Clara H. Harris, he became mentally ill, shot her to death, unsuccessfully attempted suicide, and spent the remainder of his life in a mental hospital.

Official Statement of Major H. R. Rathbone

District of Columbia
    County of Washington vs. Henry R. Rathbone, Major Brevet Major in the Army of the United States being duly sworn says, that on the 14th day of April Instant, at about 20 minutes past eight o'clock in the evening he, with Miss Clara H. Harris left his residence at the corner of 15th and H. Streets and joined the President and Mrs. Lincoln and went with them in their carriage to Fords Theatre in Tenth Street. The box assigned to the President is in the second tier, on the right hand side of the audience and was occupied by the President and Mrs. Lincoln, Miss Harris and this deponent and by no other person. The box is entered by passing from the front of the building in the rear of the dress circle to a small entry or passageway about eight feet in length and four feet in width. This passageway is entered by a door

which opens on the inner side. The door is so placed as to make an acute angle between it and the wall behind it on the inner side. At the inner end of this passageway is another door standing squarely across and opening into the box. On the left hand side of the passageway and very near the inner end is a third door which also opens into the box. This latter door was closed. The party entered the box through the door at the end of the passageway. The box is so constructed that it may be divided into two by a moveable partition, one of the doors described opening into each. The front of the box is about ten or twelve feet in length and in the centre of the railing is a small pillar overhung with a curtain. The depth of the box from front to rear is about nine feet. The elevation of the box above the stage including the railing is about ten or twelve feet.

When the party entered the box a cushioned arm chair was standing at the end of the box furthest from the stage and nearest the audience. This was also the nearest point to the door by which the box is entered. The President seated himself in this chair and, except that he once left the chair for the purpose of putting on his overcoat, remained so seated until he was shot. Mrs. Lincoln was seated in a chair between the President and the pillar in the centre, above described. At the opposite end of the box—that nearest the stage—were two chairs. In one of these, standing in the corner, Miss Harris was seated. At her left hand and along the wall running from that end of the box to the rear stood a small sofa. At the end of this sofa next to Miss Harris this deponent was seated, and the President, as they were sitting, was about seven or eight feet and the distance between this deponent and the door was about the same. The distance between the President as he sat and the door was about four or five feet. The door, according to the recollection of this deponent, was not closed during the evening.

When the second scene of the third act was being performed and while this deponent was intently observing the proceedings upon the stage with his back towards the door he heard the discharge of a pistol behind him and looking round saw through the smoke, a man between the door and the President. At the same time deponent heard him shout some word which deponent thinks was "Freedom." This deponent instantly sprang towards him and seised (*sic*) him. He wrested himself from the grasp and made a violent thrust at the breast of this deponent with a large knife. Deponent parried the blow by striking it up and received a wound several inches deep in his left arm between the elbow and the shoulder. The orifice of the wound is about an inch and a half in length and extends upwards towards the shoulder several inches. The man rushed to the front of the box and deponent endeavored to seise him again but only caught his clothes as he was leaping over the railing of the box. The clothes, as this deponent believes, were torn in this attempt to seise him. As he went over upon the stage, deponent cried out with a loud voice "Stop that man." Deponent then turned to the President. His position was not changed. His head was slightly bent forward and his eyes were closed. Deponent saw that he was unconscious and, supposing him mortally wounded, rushed to the door for the purpose of calling medical aid. On reaching the outer door of the passage way as above described, deponent found it barred by a heavy piece of plank, one end of which secured in the wall and the other resting against the door. It had been so securely fastened that it required considerable force to remove it. This wedge or bar was about four feet from the floor. Persons upon the outside were beating against the door for the purpose of entering. Deponent removed the bar and the door was opened. Several persons who represented themselves to be surgeons were allowed to enter. Deponent saw there Colonel Crawford and requested him to prevent other persons from entering the box. Deponent then returned to the box and found the surgeon examining the President's person. They had not yet discovered the wound. As soon as it was discovered, it was determined to remove him from the Theatre. He was carried out and this deponent then proceeded to assist Mrs. Lincoln, who was intensely excited, to leave the Theatre. On reaching the head of the stairs, deponent requested Major Potter to aid him in assisting Mrs. Lincoln across the street to the house to which the President was being conveyed. The wound which deponent had received had been bleeding very profusely and on reaching the house, feeling very faint from the loss of blood, he seated himself in the hall and soon after fainted away and was laid upon the floor. Upon the return of consciousness deponent was taken in the carriage to his residence.

In the review of the transaction it is the confident belief of this deponent that the time which elapsed between the discharge of the pistol and the time when the assassin leaped from the box did not exceed thirty seconds. Neither Mrs. Lincoln nor Miss Harris had left their seats.

H. R. Rathbone

Subscribed and sworn before me this
17th day of April, 1856 (*sic*)
A B Ollie
   Justice (indecipherable) D.C.

INTRODUCTORY NOTE—DOCUMENT IV

The following table is taken from Volume 8, *Assassination and Political Violence*, Chapter 1, page 12, Table 1. (See NOTES page 222). It lists all violent assaults on public office holders in the United States from 1835 to 1968. This volume of the staff report to the Commission on the Causes and Prevention of Violence is highly recommended to readers desiring to obtain additional in-depth information on the subject.

Chronological list of political assassinations and assaults. *

*This list represents all acts reported in the *New York Times*, and other prominent widely circulated newspapers, such as *The Washington Post*, the *Chicago Tribune*, the *St. Louis Dispatch*, etc. Also consulted were basic American histories and interpretative texts of various periods in American history, such as the Reconstruction period, the Depression of the 1930's and the pre-World War I era. It would be foolish to believe that the list prepared for Table 1 accounts for every attempted or successful assassination that has ever occurred in the United States. We are reasonably sure, however, that it accounts for every President, Senator, and Governor; and probably even for every Congressman. But the degree of certainty obviously decreases with the power and publicness of the office involved. Also, under the category "attempted," we do not include "threatening letters" or "crank phone calls"; an overt act must have been committed.

Year	Victim	Method of Attack and Result	Location of Attack	Assailant and Professed or Alleged Reason
1835	Andrew Jackson President	Attempted shooting, gun misfired	Washington, D.C.	Richard Lawrence; considered mentally unbalanced; said Jackson was ruining the country.

Chronological list of political assassinations and assaults (Continued)

1856	Charles Sumner Senator, Massachusetts	Assaulted, severely	Washington, D.C.	Congressman Preston Brooks of South Carolina; revenge for antislavery speech made by Sumner.
1857	David C. Broderick Senator, California	Shot in duel, killed	California	David S. Terry; insults over political stand on slavery and legal feud.
1865	Abraham Lincoln President	Shot, killed	Washington, D.C.	John Wilkes Booth; loyalty to the Confederacy; revenge for defeat; slavery issue.
	William H. Seward Secretary of State	Shot, wounded	Washington, D.C.	David Herold, Lewis Paine; part of Lincoln plot.
1867	G. W. Ashburn Delegate to Georgia Constitutional Convention	Shot, killed	Georgia	Unknown; 10 prominent citizens implicated in the murder of the Republican delegate during Reconstruction.
	Almon Case State senator	Shot, killed	Tennessee	Frank Farris; anti-Union guerrilla leader.
	L. Harris Hiscox Delegate to New York Constitutional Convention	Shot, killed	New York	Cole; personal affair over Cole's wife.
	J. W. C. Horne Judge, Georgia	Shot, killed	Georgia	Unknown Negro; judge shot over incident involving his son and a colored girl.
	H. W. Fowler Assistant collector of revenues	Shot, killed	Texas	D. B. Bonfoey, collector of revenues; no motives ascertained.

Year	Name	Outcome	State	Notes
	John P. Slough Chief Justice, New Mexico Territory	Shot, killed	New Mexico	Capt. William L. Rynerson; feud and insults over Rynerson's attempt to have Slough recalled.
1868	V. Chase Judge, Louisiana	Shot, killed	Louisiana	Band of Rebels; Chase was a Union man.
	Robert Gray Justice, Louisiana	Shot, killed	Louisiana	Unknown(s).
	Harrington State legislator; Pennington State senator, Alabama	Attempted shooting	Alabama	Unknown; ambushed while canvassing county together for Republican Party.
	James Hinds Representative, Arkansas	Shot, killed	Arkansas	George M. Clark; was Secretary of Democratic Committee; Hinds was campaigning for Republicans, Clark was drunk at the time of shooting.
	B. Saulet Sheriff, Caddo Parish, Louisiana	Shot, killed	Louisiana	Unknown(s).
	Samuel W. Beall ex-Lieutenant Gov- ernor, Wisconsin	Shot, killed	Montana	George M. Pinney; Beall attacked Pinney over articles Pinney wrote; acquitted as self-defense.
1869	M. McConnel State senator, Illinois	Shot, killed	Illinois	Unknown; believed to be over property litigation.

Chronological list of political assassinations and assaults (Continued)

Year	Name	Method	Location	Details
	Benjamin Ayers State legislator, Georgia	Shot, killed	Georgia	Wilson; robbery believed motive
1870	William S. Lincoln Representative, New York	Cane assault	Maryland	Joseph Segar; lost contested seat for Representative from Virginia
	John W. Stevens State senator, North Carolina	Stabbed, hung, killed	North Carolina	Wiley and Mitchelle, apparently acted with consent of Democratic Party of Caswell County; Stevens was a Republican.
	Gaylord Clark District Judge, Texas	Shot, killed	Texas	Frank William; sought judgeship for himself.
	A. P. Crittedon Judge, California	Shot, killed	California	Laura D. Fair, his mistress, when he attempted to break off relationship.
1871	Alden McLaughlin Customs Inspector, Texas	Shot, killed	Texas	Smugglers; in the line of duty.
1873	William Pitt Kellog Governor, Louisiana	Attempted shooting	Louisiana	Charles R. Rainey, Melvin H. Cohen; many disputed his election, open rebellion in parts of Louisiana.
	Samuel Clark Pomeroy ex-Senator, Kansas	Shot, wounded	Washington, D.C.	M. F. Conway; both men had been in Kansas politics at statehood; Conway blamed Pomeroy for his circumstances.

Year	Name / Office	Outcome	State	Notes
	T. S. Crawford District County Judge Arthur H. Harris District Attorney, Monroe, Louisiana	Shot, killed	Louisiana	Assumed to have been ambushed by the Tom Wayne gang, with whom both had previously been involved in a case.
	Edwin S. McCook Territorial Secretary of Dakota	Shot, killed	Dakota Territory	P. P. Wintermute; dispute over railroad bonds.
	H. P. Farrow U.S. District Attorney, Georgia	Clubbed, wounded	Georgia	Unknown; had got indictments against five men; papers ranted against him and tried to intimidate jury.
1874	James O'Brian ex-State senator, New York	Attempted shooting	New York	Richard Croker, George and Henry Hickey, John Sheridan; Tammany group dispute with O'Brian.
1875	E. G. Johnson Deputy Collector of Internal Revenue and State legislator, Florida	Shot, killed	Florida	Unknown(s); shot in still house.
	Belden ex-Parish Judge, Louisiana	Shot, killed	Louisiana	Sherburn; was judge at time; motive unknown.
	Daniel O'Connell Alderman, New York	Gun threat	New York	John T. Cox; personal matter over Cox's sister.
	G. A. Roderty Tax Collector, Grant Parish, Louisiana	Shot, killed	Louisiana	John B. McCoy, ex-sheriff.

Chronological list of political assassinations and assaults (*Continued*)

1877	Stephen B. Packard Governor, Louisiana	Shot, wounded	Louisiana	W. H. Weldon; apparently part of group that challenged legality of election.
1881	James A. Garfield President	Shot, killed	Maryland	Charles Guiteau; wanted political appointment.
	Smith State senator, Tennessee	Shot, wounded	Tennessee	John J. Vertress; political feud over way Smith voted; Vertress claimed Smith was bribed.
1885	John B. Bowman ex-Mayor, East St. Louis, Illinois	Shot, killed	Illinois	Unknown; previous attempts made after several men killed in Republican-Democratic clashes at City Hall during his term.
1889	Stephen J. Field Supreme Court Judge	Assaulted	California	David S. Terry; had threatened Field in legal dispute.
	David S. Terry Judge, California	Shot, killed	California	David Nagel, U.S. deputy marshal assigned to guard Field, shot and killed Terry.
	W. L. Pierce Superior Judge, San Diego, California	Shot, wounded	California	W. S. Clendennin; because of unfavorable decision handed down by Pierce.
1890	William P. Taulbee ex-Representative, Kentucky	Shot, killed	Washington	Charles E. Kincaide; feud over articles Kincaide wrote linking Taulbee to scandal; Kincaide acquitted.

214

Year	Name	Action	State	Description
1892	R. D. McCotter State senator, North Carolina	Shot, killed	North Carolina	Unknown; assumed to be personal; wife's family did not like his behavior.
1893	Carter H. Harrison Mayor, Chicago, Illinois	Shot, killed	Illinois	Patrick E. Prendergast; disappointed officeseeker.
	Henry S. Tyler Mayor, Louisville, Kentucky	Threatened with gun	Kentucky	P. J. Schwartz; did not want city limits extended to his property.
1896	Col. Albert Jennings Fountain ex-State legislator, New Mexico Territory	Shot, killed	New Mexico	Unknown; long conflict between cattle association and outlaws backed by opposite political party.
1900	William Goebel Governor, Kentucky	Shot, killed	Kentucky	Caleb Powers; tried and convicted of conspiracy; disputed election.
1901	William McKinley President	Shot, killed	New York	Leon F. Czolgosz; anarchist ideology.
1905	Frank Steunenberg ex-Governor, Idaho	Dynamite killed	Idaho	Harry Orchard; labor union against which Governor called out troops involved.
1908	John F. Fort Governor, New Jersey	Attempted bombing	New Jersey	Unknown; suspect either crackpot or parties angered by liquor law enforcement.
1910	William Gaynor Mayor, New York City	Shot, wounded	New York	John J. Gallagher; fired from city job, angered at Gaynor's trip.

Chronological list of political assassinations and assaults (Continued)

1912	Theodore Roosevelt President	Shot, wounded	Wisconsin	John Schrank; had vision that McKinley wanted him to avenge his death; Schrank declared insane.
1913	B. P. Windsor Mayor, Mt. Aubcorn, Illinois	Shot, killed	Illinois	Fay D. State; quarrel over editorial
1917	Henry Cabot Lodge Senator, Massachusetts	Assaulted	Washington, D.C.	Pacifists: A. Bannwart, Rev. P. H. Drake, Mrs. M. A. Peabody, outbursts because he did not support staying out of war; not serious attempt on life.
1921	Charles Henderson Senator, Nevada	Shot, wounded	Washington, D.C.	August Grock; personal quarrel over money.
1924	Robert Young Thomas, Jr. Representative, Kentucky	Assaulted	Kentucky	G. Baker; political opponent; Baker angered by Thomas' remarks.
1926	Jeff Stone Mayor, Culp, Illinois	Shot, killed	Illinois	Unknown; suspected political gangster bootlegging tie-in.
1933	Franklin Delano Roosevelt President	Attempted shooting	Florida	Giuseppe Zangara; hated rulers and capitalists.
	Anton Cermak Mayor, Chicago, Illinois	Shot, killed	Florida	Cermak was hit in hail of bullets aimed at Roosevelt.

Year	Name	Method	Location	Details
1935	Huey P. Long Senator, Louisiana	Shot, killed	Louisiana	Dr. Carl Weiss; apparent concern over Long's power, and having his father-in-law's judgeship taken away.
	Thomas J. Courtney State's attorney, Illinois	Shot, killed	Illinois	Unknown; suspected Capone gang.
1936	J. M. Bolton State legislator, Illinois	Shot, killed	Illinois	Assumed to be gangsters; alliance of crime and politics.
1939	Louis E. Edwards Mayor, Long Beach, New York	Shot, killed	New York	Alvin Dooley; angered that Edwards used influence to keep him from being elected to office in police organization.
1945	Warren G. Hooper State senator, Michigan	Shot, killed	Michigan	Conspirators: Harry and Sam Fleisher, Mike Selik, Pete Mahoney; Hooper had been key witness in an investigation.
1947	John William Bricker Senator, Ohio	Shot, wounded	Washington, D.C.	William L. Kaiser; personal grudge over money lost when Bricker was attorney general.
	Hubert H. Humphrey Mayor, Minneapolis, Minnesota	Attempted shooting	Minnesota	Unknown; several attempts made; conflicts over crime-labor unions.
	Thomas Anglin State senator, Oklahoma	Shot, wounded	Oklahoma	Jim Scott; personal; Anglin's law firm represented Scott's wife in divorce.

Chronological list of political assassinations and assaults (Continued)

1949	Elihu H. Bailey Mayor, Evarts, Kentucky	Attempted dynamite	Kentucky	Unknown; mayor thought it was bootlegger he was fighting.
1950	Harry S Truman President	Attempted shooting	Washington, D.C.	Oscar Collazo, Griselio Torresola; Puerto Rican Independence.
1954	Kenneth Allison Roberts Representative, Alabama Benton Franklin Jensen Representative, Iowa George Hyde Fallon Representative, Maryland Alvin Morell Bentley Representative, Michigan Clifford Davis Representative, Tennessee	Shot, wounded	Washington, D.C.	Puerto Rican extremists: Lolita Lebron, Rafael Cancel Miranda, A. F. Corcera; attack on Congress by inde- pendence group.
1958	Paul A. Wallace State senator, South Carolina	Shot, killed	South Carolina	Henry Rogers; assumed mad, hanged self in mental institution.
1959	J. Lindsay Almond, Jr. Governor, Virginia	Attempted shooting	Virginia	Unknown; suspected segrega- tionist; during school integration period.
1963	John F. Kennedy President	Shot, killed	Texas	Lee Harvey Oswald; motivation unknown.

John Connally Governor, Texas	Shot, wounded	Texas	Lee Harvey Oswald; accident assuming assassin was aiming at President.
1968 Robert F. Kennedy, Senator, New York	Shot, killed	California	Sirhan Sirhan, accused; foreign policy statements vis à vis the Middle East.

INTRODUCTORY NOTE–DOCUMENT V

From Volume 8, *Assassination and Political Violence*, Chapter 1, page 20, Table 2. (See NOTES, Page 222).

Likelihood of assassination by type of public office
(1790–1968)

OFFICE	NUMBER OF MAN TERMS	ESTIMATES OF THE NUMBER HOLDING OFFICE	NUMBER OF ASSASSINATIONS ATTEMPTED	PERCENTAGE OF UNIVERSALITY
President	45	35	8[b]	23
Governors[a]	1,710	1,330	8	00.6
Senators[a]	2,271	1,140	8[c]	00.7
Representatives[a]	27,930	8,349	9	00.1

[a] Number of man terms was computed from apportionment census material listed in *Biographical Directory of the American Congress 1774–1961* (Reynolds U.S. Government Printing Office.) The Representatives were multiplied by 5 indicating five terms per decade, the Senators by 1.67. The Governors were computed by the number of States in the Union for each census period and then multiplying by 2.5. The figure for estimated Governors actually served was computed by taking 77.8 percent man terms—the same as that for President. The Senators are based on an average of 0.81 per page and Congressmen 5.93 per page for 1,408 pages in the biographical sketch section of the above-cited volume.

[b] Includes Theodore Roosevelt, an ex-President who was also a presidential candidate.

[c] Includes Senator Robert Kennedy who was also presidential candidate.

220

NOTES

CHAPTER I

1. *History of the Assassins* by Joseph von Hammer-Purgstall, translated from the German by Oswald Charles Wood, M.D., Smith & Elder, Cornhill, London, 1835. Page 11
2. *ibid.* Page 34
3. *History of the Order of the Assassins* by Enno Franzius, Funk & Wagnalls, New York, 1969
4. *Memoir of the Order of the Assassins, and on the Origin of their Name* by Sylvestre de Sacy, read at the public meeting of the Institute of France, July 7, 1809, reprinted in *Le Moniteur,* Paris, July 29, 1809 (translated by O. C. Wood, M.D.; reprinted in English in von Hammer-Purgstall *op. cit.,* page 234)
5. *The Polytechnic Journal,* London, September, 1840, quoted by F. Hollick in *Murder Made Moral; Or An Account Of The Thugs And Other Secret Murderers of India,* Manchester, England, 18—. Pages 6–8

CHAPTER II

1. Xenophon, *Hiero,* IV, 5, in *Scripta Minora,* Loeb Classical Library ed., 1925. Page 27. (The use of the word "assassins" in the quote is not precisely accurate, since Xenophon died before the word came into use.)

2. *The Histories of Polybius,* trans. by E. S. Schuckburgh, London, 1889. Vol. I, page 155
3. *De Officiis,* III, 4, quoted in *Against the Tyrant,* by Oscar Jaszi and John D. Lewis, The Free Press, Glencoe, Illinois, 1957. Page 10
4. *A History of the Italian Republics* by J. C. L. de Sismondi (one-volume ed.), London, 1832. Page 88
5. *The Renaissance and Its Makers* by J. D. Symon & S. L. Bensusan, T. C. & E. C. Jack, London, 1913. Page 97
6. *Obras,* II, Juan de Mariana. Page 468

CHAPTER III

1. *Famous Assassinations of History* by Francis Johnson, Chicago, 1903. Pages 19–20
2. Quoted by Johnson *op. cit.* Pages 221–2
3. *op.cit.* Page 223.
4. *Memoirs,* Catherine II, quoted by Jesse D. Clarkson in *A History of Russia,* Random House, 2nd edition, 1962. Page 240
5. Johnson *op.cit.* Page 312.
6. *The Fall of Dynasties, The Collapse of the Old Order, 1905–1922* by Edmund Taylor, Doubleday, New York, 1963. Page 14

CHAPTER IV

1. Clarkson *op. cit.* Page 492
2. *Assassination and Political Violence,* Volume 8 of the Staff Report to the National Commission on the Causes and Prevention of Violence, prepared by James F. Kirkham, Sheldon Levy, and William J. Crotty, Government Printing Office, Washington, D.C., 1969. (Supplement A, *Political Violence and Terror in 19th and 20th Century Russia and Eastern Europe* by Feliks Gross, pages 459–60.)
3. Quoted by Joseph Bornstein, *The Politics of Murder,* William Sloane Associates Inc., New York, 1950. Page 122
4. *Heydrich: Hitler's Most Evil Henchman* by Charles Wighton, Odhams Press, London, 1962. Page 26
5. *To The Bitter End* by Hans Bernd Gisevius, translated by Richard & Clara Winston, Houghton Mifflin Company, Boston, 1947. Page 50
6. *Gestapo, Instrument of Tyranny* by Edward Crankshaw, Viking Press, New York, 1956.

7. From the official transcript of the Nuremberg Trials, as quoted by Crankshaw *op.cit.*
8. Quoted by Crankshaw *op.cit.*

CHAPTER V

All direct quotes and extracts in this chapter are taken from journals and newspapers of the time (*The Atlas* n.d., *John Bull,* London, March 6, 1843, and *The Times* of London, Jan. 21, 1843, Jan. 27, 1843, and March 4, 1843).

CHAPTER VI

1. *The Web of Conspiracy* by Theodore Roscoe, Prentice-Hall, Inc., Englewood Cliffs, N. J., 1959.
2. *History of the United States Secret Service* by Lafayette C. Baker, privately published, Philadelphia, 1867. Revised edition, John E. Potter & Co., Philadelphia, 1889.
3. *The Life, Crime, and Capture of J. W. Booth* by George Alfred Townsend, Dick & Fitzgerald, New York, 1865.
4. *Perley's Reminiscences* by Ben Perley Poore, Hubbard Brothers, Philadelphia, 1886.
5. *Anatomy of an Assassination* by John Cottrell, Frederick Muller, London, 1966.

CHAPTER VII

1. *The Hired Killers* by Peter Wyden, William Morrow & Company, New York, 1963. Page 7
2. *Murder, Inc., The Story of "The Syndicate"* by Burton B. Turkus and Sid Feder, Farrar, Strauss & Young, New York, 1951 (from Introduction by Sid Feder, page xiii).
3. *ibid.* Page 8

CHAPTER VIII

1. *Assassination and Political Violence,* Volume 8 *op. cit.* (Supplement F, *Assassination in the Middle East,* Part 3, by Carl Leiden. Page 549.)
2. *The Davos Murder* by Emil Ludwig, translated by Eden and Cedar Paul, Viking Press, New York, 1936 (quoting from contemporary newspaper reports from Chur, Switzerland). Pages 92–93

3. *Assassination and Political Violence,* Volume 8 *op.cit.* Pages 2–3
4. *Assassination and Political Violence,* Volume 8 *op.cit.* Page 3
5. *ibid.* (Feliks Gross, page 422.)
6. *General Sherman and Total War* by John B. Walters in *Journal of Southern History,* November, 1948. Pages 447–480
7. *Assassination and Political Violence,* Volume 8 *op.cit.* Page 3
8. *ibid.* Page 4
9. *Kilmainham Memories* by Tighe Hopkins, *Windsor Magazine,* London, 1896.
10. Quoted by Edward Hyams in *Killing No Murder,* Thomas Nelson & Sons, Ltd., London, 1969. Page 182

CHAPTER IX

1. *Assassination and Political Violence,* Volume 8 *op.cit.* (Appendix B, page 291.)
2. *ibid.* Page 292
3. *ibid.* Pages 292–3
4. *Why the United States leads the world in the relative proportion of murders, lynchings and other felonies, and why the Anglo-Saxon countries not under the American Flag have the least proportion of murders and felonies and know no lynchings.* A paper, read before the Society of Medical Jurisprudence, New York City, December 11, 1916 by Henry A. Forster.

CHAPTER X

1. Quoted by Robert Baldick in *The Duel,* Chapman & Hall, London, 1965. Page 120
2. Quoted by C. L. Douglas in *Famous Texas Feuds,* The Turner Company, Dallas, 1936. Page 47
3. *ibid.* (Introduction.)
4. All quotes attributed to General William T. Sherman from *Journal of Southern History op. cit.* and *Sherman and the South* by E. Merton Coulter, *Georgia Historical Quarterly,* 1931, Vol. 15, pages 28–45
5. *Poine, A Study in Ancient Greek Blood Vengeance* by Hubert J. Treston, Longmans, Green & Company, London, 1923. Page 1
6. Anon. 18th century, quoted by B. J. Hurwood in *Torture Through the Ages,* Paperback Library, New York, 1969.

7. Thomas Paine: Letter addressed to: "My Fellow Citizens," Luxembourg, 8th of Pluvoise in the Second Year of the French Republic.
8. Story by David Burnham in *The New York Times,* Sunday, April 20, 1969
9. Edward Hyams *op.cit.* (Introduction, page 10.)
10. Voltaire: *Dictionnaire Philosophique,* On War, 1764
11. Quoted in *The Great Quotations,* compiled by George Seldes, Lyle Stuart, New York, 1960. Page 540 (Pocket Book ed., May, 1967.)

BIBLIOGRAPHY

(Books and periodicals cited in the *Notes* are not repeated here)

Bailey, Geoffrey   *The Conspirators,* New York, 1960

Barrett, J. G.   *Sherman's March through the Carolinas,* Chapel Hill, N.C., 1956

Bishop, Jim   *The Day Lincoln Was Shot,* New York, 1955

deFord, Miriam Allen   *Murderers Sane & Mad,* London, New York, Toronto, 1965

Dewar, Hugo   *Assassins at Large,* London, 1951

Donovan, Robert J.   *The Assassins,* New York, 1952

Durant, Will & Ariel   *The Age of Reason Begins (The Story of Civilization: Part VII*), New York, 1961

Eisenschiml, Otto   *Why Was Lincoln Murdered?,* New York, 1939

Fattorusso, Joseph & Rita *Kings & Queens of England & France* (2 vols.), Florence, 1953, 1954

Forrester, Izola   *This One Mad Act; The Unknown Story of John Wilkes Booth,* Boston, 1937

Graham, Hugh Davis & Gurr, Ted Robert   *Violence In America; Historical & Comparative Perspectives* (Volumes 1 & 2, Staff Report to the National Commission on the Causes & Prevention of Violence), Washington, D.C., 1969

Hermel, Hans Peter   *Jagdgeschwader Horst Wessel* (etc.), Berlin, 1938

Hibbert, Christopher   *The Roots of Evil,* Boston, Toronto, 1963

Hurwood, Bernhardt J.   *Torture Through the Ages,* New York, 1969

Johnson, Lewis F.   *Famous Kentucky Tragedies & Trials,* Louisville, 1916

Kardorff, Ursula von   *Diary of a Nightmare,* London, 1965

Kessel, Joseph   *The Man with the Miraculous Hands,* New York, 1961

Kimmel, Stanley   *The Mad Booths of Maryland,* New York, 1940

Lewis, Bernard   *The Assassins,* New York, 1968

Lewis, Lloyd   *Sherman, Fighting Prophet,* New York, 1932

Loomis, Stanley   *Paris in the Terror,* New York, 1964

Lüdecke, Winfried   *Behind the Scenes of Espionage,* London, 1929

Manvell, Roger & Fraenkell, Heinrich   *Dr. Goebbels: His Life and Death,* New York, 1961

Masters, John   *The Deceivers,* New York, 1952

Neumann, Peter   *Other Men's Graves* (Translated by Constantine Fitz Gibbon), London, 1959

Nichols, George Ward   *Story of the Great March,* New York, 1865

Oldenbourg, Zoe   *Massacre at Montségur, A History of the Albigensian Crusade* (translated by Peter Green), New York, 1962

Polo, Marco   *Kingdoms & Marvels of the East* (Volume 1) (translated by Henry Yule), New York, 1903

Prezzolini, Giuseppe   *Machiavelli* (translated by Gioconda Savini, from *The Italian, Machiavelli Anticristo*), New York, 1967

Scott, James B.   *The Catholic Conception of International Law,* Washington, D.C., 1934

Scottish League For European Freedom   *The Crime of Moscow in Vynntsia,* Edinburgh, 1952

Seth, Ronald   *The Executioners,* New York, 1968

Shirer, William L.   *The Rise and Fall of the Third Reich,* New York, 1960

Sparrow, Judge Gerald   *The Great Assassins,* New York, 1968

Suarez, Francisco *Selections from the Works of Francisco Suarez, S. J. (Classics of International Law, Volume II,* prepared by Gladys L. Williams, Ammi Brown and John Waldron, with certain revision by Henry Davis, S. J. and an Introduction by James Brown Scott), London, 1944

Tresca Memorial Committee *Who Killed Carlo Tresca?,* New York, 1945

Tuchman, Barbara W. *The Guns of August,* New York, 1962

Ulam, Adam B. *The Bolsheviks,* New York, 1965

Willey, Peter *The Castles of the Assassins,* London, 1963

Williams, John *Heyday for Assassins,* London, 1958

Williams, Neville *Chronology of the Modern World,* New York, 1967

Williamson, Hugh Ross *Historical Whodunits,* New York, 1956

Wolfe, Lawrence *A Short History of Russia,* London, n.d.

NEWSPAPERS, PERIODICALS, ENCYCLOPEDIAS, AND JOURNALS

The Atlas (London)

Encyclopaedia Britannica, 11th Ed. (London & New York, 1910–1911)

British Medical Journal (Jan. 14, 1956, pages 107–108)

John Bull (London, March 6, 1843)

Journal of the House of Lords (London, June 19, 1843)

Lancet (London, 1843 & 1904)

New York (April 6, 1970)

New York Herald (Nov. 12, 1864 to Dec. 21, 1864)

New York Times (Nov. 12, 1864 to Dec. 21, 1864 and current issues)

New York Post (current)

The Saturday Review (London, Aug. 1, 1874)

The Times of London (Jan. 21, 1843; Jan. 27, 1843; March 4, 1843)

234

Mornard, Jacques, 68–69
Moslems, 4, 5, 45
Mowaffek, 7, 8
Moyne, Lord, assassination of, 150
Mudd, Dr. Samuel A., 110, 116, 117
Mueller, Heinrich, 75
Munich, trial in, 74
Munro, Dr., 102
Münster, Count, and assassination of Paul I, 53
murder: as political tool, 2; and judicial process, 60–61
Murder, Inc., 129, 138; and Dewey, 130–132; and assassination, 135–136
Murder, Inc., 129
Mussolini, Benito, 57, 58
MVD, 67

Napier, Sir Charles James, on Americans and Negroes, 181
Nasser, Gamal Abdel, attempted assassination of, 63
National Commission on the Causes and Prevention of Violence: report of, 62–63; on categories of assassination, 141–142, 146, 147, 150; on precursors to assassinations, 151; tables from reports of, 209–220
National Socialism, 63; and assassination, 69–80; emergence and slogan of, 69
National Socialist White People's Party, *see* American Nazi Party
Nazis, *see* National Socialism
Neff, Roy, 122
Nero, 22, 23
Newton, Huey, and weapons, 155
New York Magazine, interview in, 156
New York *Post,* 160
New York *Times:* Reuter's dispatch in, 157; on Arabs and RFK assassination, 163
Nicholas I of Russia, 54

Nihilists, 54
Nishapur, 7
Nizam-al-Mulk, 7
Nizar, assassination of, 9
NKVD, 67
Nuremberg Trials, 79, 80

O'Banion, Dion, 133
OGPU, 67
Okhrana, 64, 65
O'Laughlin, Michael, 109, 110, 116, 117
Old Man of the Mountain, The, 10; excerpts from, 189–201
Olgiati, Girolamo, 26, 27
Olympias, 41, 42, 43
Omar Khayyam, 7
Ommiad caliphate, 7
On A Late Acquittal, 103–104
Orloff, Alexis, 49, 50, 51
Orloff, Gregor, 49
Oswald, Lee Harvey, 105, 158, 162
Othman, Caliph, assassination of, 45
Our American Cousin, 113

Paine, Lewis, 109–112, 115–117
Paine, Thomas, quote from, 182
Palestine, terrorism in, 144, 149
Parker, John F., 114–115
Partridge, James, 87
Patterson, Mrs., 97
Paul, son of Catherine the Great, 49
Paul I of Russia, assassination of, 53
Paul V, Pope, 30
Paul, Saint, quote from, 22, 23
Pausanius, 43
Pearl Harbor, 58
Peel, Sir Robert, 82, 86, 90, 98, 105
Persians, 7
Peter, Saint, quote from, 22
Peter III of Russia, 47–51, 53; assassination of, 50–51
Phansigars, *see* Thugs
Philip II of Macedon, 41–43

238

PICTURE CREDITS

Pictures 1, 2, 3, 5, 6, 8, 10, 11, 16, 19 through 22 and 33 through 43 are from the picture collection of the New York Public Library; pictures 4, 7, 12, and 13 are from The Bettmann Archive; pictures 9, 15, 17, and 18 are from *Famous Assassinations of History* by Francis Johnson; pictures 14, 46, 47, 63, 64, and 65 are from Culver Studios; pictures 23, 24, 25, 48, 49, 50, 53, 61, and 62 are from Wide World Photos; pictures 26, 27, 28, 51, 52, and 54 through 60 are from United Press International (UPI); pictures 29, 30, and 31 are from Radio Times Hulton Picture Library (British Broadcasting Corporation), London, England; pictures 32, 44, and 45 are from the Library of Congress.